LETTERS FROM A LIVING UTOPIA

RECLAIMING LIBERATION FROM
PALESTINE TO THE WORLD

LETTERS FROM A LIVING UTOPIA
RECLAIMING LIBERATION FROM
PALESTINE TO THE WORLD

Yaffa AS

Brooklyn, NY
Philadelphia, PA
commonnotions.org

Letters from a Living Utopia: Reclaiming Liberation
from Palestine to the World
© Yaffa AS
This edition © 2025 Common Notions

This work is licensed under the Creative Commons Attribution-NonCommercial 4.0 International. To view a copy of this license, visit https://creativecommons.org/licenses/by-nc/4.0/

ISBN: 978-1-945335-30-3 | eBook ISBN: 978-1-945335-69-3
Library of Congress Number: 2025944447

10 9 8 7 6 5 4 3 2 1

Common Notions
c/o Interference Archive
314 7th St.
Brooklyn, NY 11215

Common Notions
c/o Making Worlds Bookstore
210 S. 45th St.
Philadelphia, PA 19104

www.commonnotions.org
info@commonnotions.org

Discounted bulk quantities of our books are available for organizing, educational, or fundraising purposes. Please contact Common Notions at any of the addresses above for more information.

Cover design by Josh MacPhee
Layout design and typesetting by Sydney Rainer

CONTENTS

Preface   1
Suleiman Y.

Introduction   5
Yaffa

LETTER ONE
23/Leo/23   11
Dear Yaffa (as you await liberation)

LETTER TWO
17/Leo/6   27
Dear Suleiman

LETTER THREE
28/Virgo/7   35
Dear Dana

LETTER FOUR
20/Sagittarius/4   39
Dear Liberation

LETTER FIVE
5/Aries/12   47
Dear Reem

LETTER SIX
8/Cancer/26   57
Dear Home

LETTER SEVEN
27/Pisces/16   65
Dear Rest

LETTER EIGHT
28/Leo/32
Dear Little One
73

LETTER NINE
19/Aquarius/1
Dear Malak
85

LETTER TEN
13/Libra/17
To everyone who has harmed me
97

LETTER ELEVEN
5/Scorpio/3
Dear Hawa & Rakan
105

LETTER TWELVE
25/Gemini/22
Dear Beloved Language
113

LETTER THIRTEEN
2/Taurus/25
Dear Mama
119

LETTER FOURTEEN
23/Scorpio/32
Dear Death
133

LETTER FIFTEEN
3/Capricorn/33
Dear Yaffa
141

About the Author
149

About Common Notions
151

Preface

When I had asked Yaffa to compile a set of letters from their extensive collection, I was not ready for what arrived, neatly packaged and only sent to me after they had returned home to Falasteen. Our archive houses thousands of records from the years before liberation and after, and recently I have been focusing on acquiring letters, stories, and memorabilia from our elders—specifically items of theirs that were not already in circulation, that they'd never sent, or had not been passed down to others prior to their return home. These letters are then compiled along with others that have been passed down, giving us a glimpse into intimate and unspoken choices made at the time of what to keep to themself and what they gifted others.

I hesitated to ask Yaffa, for I knew that they would tell me that their voice has been on tens of thousands of pages of literature and would go on and on about the joy in witnessing other voices. I would roll my eyes through some of those conversations from my childhood, but as a child raised partially by Yaffa, I selfishly wanted more of them.

There is no number of words that can adequately represent a person's life, nor would I want them to, but still I wanted the world to witness Yaffa as they aged, in a way that I have been fortunate to. They hadn't published in over two decades and even then, it was mostly interviews and not new writing. I sent them my request, and I am honored that they agreed.

The letters were received in the order they are presented in, though knowing Yaffa and their work, the arrangement is open to the reader to bring their own magic and interpretations into them. In my own experience reading these letters, they feel like a portrait of and a portal to Yaffa and all that they are, to the Yaffa before liberation, the person who is a caretaker, who is made by their community and family, the spirit healer, the inner child, the Yaffa who has been harmed immensely, the one who is love, who is dying, who is liberated, and of course, with their intense love for their land, Yaffa, the place they are named after. Each letter shows a different vision of the world we live in, not as something external, but rather an extension of ourselves in which we are a complete circuit with land and spirit.

Included in this print collection and gallery are the fifteen letters from Yaffa directly, entirely unedited, with a brief introduction they included.

Preface 3

Without further ado, I hand you off to one of my most cherished loved ones, Yaffa.

Suleiman Y.
Director of Archives
Mahfuthat Al-Yasmeen
Al-Khayriyya, Falasteen
23 Cancer 33

Introduction

I have written thousands of letters throughout my life, starting at age seventeen. I wrote letters when it felt like the world was falling apart, initially through houselessness, hunger, and suicidality. I wrote letters when I felt immense joy. I wrote letters when I felt inspired. I wrote letters when I felt devastated and demotivated. I wrote letters as a practice to connect with myself and the extensions of everything else that is beyond me. I wrote to friends and family, community and strangers, but to be honest I wrote mostly to the beings I could not have a verbal conversation with; to practices, land, spirit, culture, concepts, and ways of being. There are spiritual traditions that claim we make gods from everything around us. Similarly, I find myself yearning to connect with the facets of a universe

I can barely comprehend. I talk to God often; I always have and always will. I also talk to everything in creation, and as you will likely find here, letters and meditations have long been my way of communing with The Divine.

Even when my letters are directed to individuals, they are rarely received by the addressee, for these letters are for specific people in a specific pocket of time and place and they do not exist beyond these shared memories. The same applies to the practices I speak to, to liberation and death, for instance, and even to the land in the final letter in this collection. The shared connection between us in a letter exists momentarily, constantly evolving.

I have always been inspired by Palestinian letter writing and the power it carries of recounting our lives, particularly falling in love with Fadwa Touqan's collection of letters to the sister of her lover. These letters inspired me to use the medium as a way to process, to conceive of new ideas, to share life, to share grief, and to map out the past and the future.

In the time of our ancestors, letters were how we communicated with one another, a form of writing that encapsulated the special duality of time in its relationality, where the distance between sender and receiver is suddenly closed upon arrival and a new connection, uniquely intimate, is forged; yet often this process might involve a month of waiting in transit as thoughts move across long distances, their meaning acquiring a sense of history in motion both extraordinary and mundane. In my world communicating with letters was never a necessity, it was a gift, a gift that would honor a moment in time that had passed, to preserve it for oneself and the letter's recipient, knowing no preservation is possible as new memories, events, and desires swirl around all relics

Introduction 7

of the present as they slip in the past. These letters illustrate my attempt at living in a more liberated time, in which the past, present, and future are always in the making, worlds now shape worlds to come, and vice versa.

I have often preferred to send short messages to my loved ones letting them know of the love we share. In this regard, there is very little in these letters that those around me have not heard before, and even if they have forgotten under the weight of new memories, they are not new. I leave very few surprises when I return home. I leave these letters as a form of remembrance, as a reminder that we have lived and we have loved, that the world is made by and for us. A reminder that living and loving are practices of labor in service of land, spirit, and others. These letters cover about three decades of my collective life. I deliberated whether to add letters from before we lived in a liberated world, but those letters are of a different time for a different archive to be recreated.

I haven't desired for my writings to be published these last several years, but in the meantime, my notebooks have filled an entire bookshelf. My intention has been to center others in the process of writing through our liberation—and that is the primary reason. But there is another, which represents a continuation of my culture work throughout the decades. I have often been asked to write and speak about how liberation happened, to narrate how we moved from point A to point B as if our liberation was a single event or linear unfolding. I refuse to anchor us in that kind of attachment. I can tell you what all of us know, how everything escalated as the UN fell not because we organized against it but because the same colonizing states who created it could no longer brand it as anything but a weapon used to further the colonial project. I can tell you how the EU was destabilized by its interminable economic crises and rampant border regimes; once those borders were effectively dismantled by the movement of migrants and refugees, it destabilized the borders of every settler colony. I can tell you about the countless revolutions, about everyone and everything we lost and gained, I can tell you about the land still recovering decades later.

I can tell you about how the genocide in Gaza spilled over into the region, how people mobilized and how they tore each other apart due to transphobia, ableism, and Islamophobia, and then I can tell you about how they came together, Syria and Türkiye on fire, bombs raining in Amman, and how there were no other options. I can tell you that Falasteen was freed and we almost lost the rest of the world when so many believed it was all over. I can tell you about how it wasn't, about the concentration camps on every continent and how they spurred riots, and when those riots became mutual aid, they became revolutions. The revolutions led to practice. Practice led to a new world.

I can tell you a lot, but I will also say again and again that those were not the things that led to liberation and allowed us to live in this world. Liberation is a practice, not an event. Until the world learned to be liberated, it was not. Some systems, built for domination and attachment, fell in flames. Others were built with vision and practice—those flourished.

We began building this world the moment systems of oppression were birthed, and the work continues to this day, even as we celebrate our liberation. It took us time to understand this and from time to time there is a push to return to wanting easy answers, as if knowing the future has ever led to it or made the work of getting there any easier.

Introduction 9

To have a perfect nonattached practice is to reach enlightenment, and if we all reach enlightenment then there would be no more growth, life would end as we know it. As such, when we sense a threat to our security we yearn to attach to outcomes, and many want to know how we got here, hoping that a single answer will return that security to them. Was it the sanitation workers' strikes in Philadelphia that led to everyone leaving trash in front of every police precinct, to barricade the streets against ICE officers and vigilantes for months leading to enough street fighting, mutual aid initiatives, and overall destabilization, that hundreds—and then thousands—of city halls and city centers were taken over and converted into spaces of life instead of oppression? Was it the mutual aid networks, the accountability hubs, the deconstructed schooling, the collective kitchens, solidarity health clinics, and neighborhood assemblies? Was it the fall of the US empire like everyone thought it would be? Was it Falasteen tasting freedom and realizing that a single place is not enough? Different answers exist for different people, depending on where they stood and the work they did.

Mama thinks it was the student movement. I believe it was when there was a reckoning across every movement to truly be a movement for Indigenous sovereignty and centered trans and disabled bodies as immediate expressions of that sovereignty. But that was years before the collective liberation that the masses agree on. There is no one answer to serve as blueprint, the work just happened within us and when it does then it creates the map for the future like it did then and does today.

Fear is a beautiful emotion, reminding us of who we are. We remember who we are by living, not by reliving memories decades old and the nostalgic action we took as we departed from a world that never let us live, into the one we continue to build today. It is easy to pretend there is one action that will solve it all, but we know in reality that our lives are infinitely more complicated, and there are no shortcuts to living our lives in a practice of liberation. We are the stitches of a liberated world. We learned that when a single stitch is pulled it threatens the entire world, and we learned to weave together, to build brighter and more intricate patterns guiding us like a map. We learned to heal, to hope, to love, to witness, to move . . . to live, with dignity. That built utopia. Those practices are what led to the strikes and riots, to the assemblies and popular committees, and they are what led to the care to nurture us into a new world—not the other way around. For us to be able to understand the revolutionary role of violence—how to infiltrate, set fire, and even assassinate—we had to learn to live liberated lives first. We wasted a lot in the process until we learned this fact.

I share these letters as a gift, releasing them from any possible outcomes. I release them like I release every memory and every attachment to this life. What you do with them from here is your decision, not mine. May you find the wisdom you need, always, in these letters and in every part of life. May you always practice liberation.

Until we meet at home,
The one who was once named after the City of Oranges

LETTER ONE
23/Leo/23

Dear Yaffa (as you await liberation),

I am writing you from a future you have long awaited.

As I entered adulthood, already familiar with the realities of war and displacement, houselessness and starvation, I hated myself. A hatred seeped deeply into all the spaces and parts of myself that I didn't even know, until I hated myself enough that I kept myself alive out of spite, thinking I wasn't worthy of death.

I remember this time like a sunset I had seen decades ago, I know what it looks like in my mind but the particulars escape me. I write this in a world where the concept of hating myself—hating myself to that degree—seems like

12   *Letters from a Living Utopia*

the climax of the worst nightmare, i.e., not of this world. But I remember it, felt to this day just under my nails, and it feels like if I scratch my skin enough this reality will be remembered and reclaimed.

It was a therapist at the time who asked what I would say to the child I was at four and at six. Those ages were not arbitrary. I had been healing from the post-traumatic stress of surviving my childhood and subsequent life surviving capitalism, and I can say with certainty that not all healing is equal. Some healing happens between multiple full-time jobs, housing and food insecurity, without friends or family. Other healing happens on a remote beach on stolen land where there is space to reflect on astrological transits post a spa day like it did in my thirties. Then, there is the healing of today, where it happens with community grounded in land and spirit, the stars transiting and sharing their wisdom along the way. This healing no longer happens hidden away from the fabric of society, rather it is integral to everything that is known as society.

I didn't know it then, but my therapist's question was the start of my inner-child journey. I was not receptive to kindness to myself at the time, a life of brutality and societies across continents that only ever told me to hate myself interfering. However, kindness to others I knew intimately and at times begrudgingly—to be able to gift kindness to everyone but yourself (even for a short period of time) is like watering every plant except for one and watching it wither away every day and telling yourself it's okay because all the other plants are well. But they are not well, they are a part of an ecosystem and when one is dying, they are all in pain, never the same (I did not know this consciously yet). Turning

Dear Yaffa (as you await liberation) 13

kindness toward a four- and six-year-old child, even myself, was easy. Even back then, my ego was not so grand that it encompassed every person I had ever been and will ever be. I am who I am in a particular moment in time, not the next or the previous—those are unique beings of their own. This understanding is now common, but it wasn't back then in the early 2010s.

Like with most other things, I took it a little further than my therapist had intended. Every day I started transforming my life, believing that someday the child would come back, would replace my consciousness, and they would thrive. I had to set them up for success. So I started saying kinder things. I started planning out who I would be around and places they could go. I started going on weekly trips, exploring, and finding them homes. Why just be kind when I can build them a universe? I laugh writing this because I marvel at how far I've come, and I love how ridiculously resilient I am.

The details of the transition from my consciousness to theirs is a bit fuzzy, but they showed up one day. About six months after this started, I saw them. I'm not sure if it was the lack of sleep or the aftermath of the Boston Marathon bombings in 2013, but as I went to the bathroom, the air mattress trying to reclaim its shape after my departure (no longer sleeping in the bathtub or closet), I saw them in the mirror.

They weren't a child anymore, not four or six, they were the age my consciousness was, somehow timeless though I was older. Their features were defined, clear skin, brilliant hazel-green eyes, hair that curled and waved as if saying hello. They looked nothing like me; they were gorgeous. I knew in that moment that they (the person I saw) were the body I lived

14   *Letters from a Living Utopia*

in but without body dysmorphia. This was what everyone else potentially saw. It made sense to my lovely autistic mind that when the child claimed the body that I would take with me a lot of the mental health challenges I grew up with. I would take everything that harmed us with me; they would have a clean slate.

I stared in the mirror for hours but then pulled away praying they'd be there when I woke up, desperately needing sleep after over forty-eight hours awake. They weren't there when I woke up.

I tried harder, thinking I just needed to do more for them. I needed to heal and transform, to build a life they would feel safe to step into.

Things changed along the way. I built the life I (in all my consciousness) could step into.

Years later, I realized they wanted a relationship, not to erase me. I still built for them and in the process, for us not just the constellation of all the different versions of me in existence, but encompassing community ecosystems of humans, land, celestial bodies, and spirit.

I know it was hard. I know it was decades of full-time jobs and abandoned beaches before the world was able to hold people like us. I send you this letter in hopes that your nervous system will settle now that you live in a liberated world. We both know that the end of oppression does not register with ease within nervous systems conditioned by a world that wanted you to struggle to survive.

I send you love from where I sit, where I love my life for you.

There will come a day when you will look in the mirror and find remnants of me, like I find remnants of you every

Dear Yaffa (as you await liberation) 15

day. You taught me to live utopia, and I merely live in a world where liberation is the lived reality. I continue your work every day, building you and everyone else a life that is worthy of your liberation.

To build you this life, where you wake up knowing how to be liberated and how to live in utopia, I attempt to live it every day. I attempt to love and belong and self-actualize and have faith and embrace the erotic and conflict and grow and grow and grow, so that you find the life you belong to.

I live utopia for you. I do not desire gratitude or acknowledgment. I know this will be repaid to community countless times over.

Someday, your inside world and outside worlds will meet, and liberation will extend beyond anything you've ever known, and you will be home.

***

I smile as I think about you at thirty-two. I am amazed and in awe of all that you are and were. Knowing all I know now, I am in awe of how you held onto a vision of utopia, even as everything around you seemed to fall apart. I remember you being in space after space, community after community reminding others that utopia was guaranteed and was meant to be lived every day, even as war, genocide, and starvation engulfed our people.

I remember with great pride how even when you felt disconnected from others you were collectivist in everything you did. You looked into night skies in a world where starlight could not reach most places. You witnessed state violence killing friends and family while communities tore into one another in an attempt to process the pain of a dying empire's

16 *Letters from a Living Utopia*

violence. You carried grief of thousands of people, names of hundreds of queer and trans people that would never be shared because the world could not carry what they did not understand. Your body ached, your mind tearing at the seams as surgeries tried to piece you back together.

You still showed up in ways defined by collectivism and a mission for liberation, while building the culture of the utopia you and everyone else deserved.

Remember the community you built at the time? The loved ones who inspired your sense of security where you realized it was something that exists between you, the land, and spirit? At a time when everyone thought you would die like so many others, you worked with communities to support them in building structures and liberatory practices that would render systems of oppression irrelevant.

I remember the devastation and ache you held in your heart, and no matter how much you asked for support, you didn't receive it except from the select few who were also never held.

I think about you at thirty-two because it was a big year. Even back then you understood it was a critical year that shifted the world. Visibly the world shifted in the first year of a second Trump presidency and fascism moved closer and closer to every community you had ever known. At the same time, you had to survive the weight of witnessing so much that even in a fascist world most people still did not see or care to see. So much was visible, yet everyone you knew was still invisible. Trans Muslim asylees and trans undocumented folks disappeared, and no one knew. Queer and trans Palestinians, Sudanese, Congolese, and Kashmiris all experienced

Dear Yaffa (as you await liberation) 17

genocide, becoming numbers without names or stories. Two-spirit Indigenous people were disappeared. That second half of thirty-two was defined by your people being disappeared and no matter how much you screamed and shared, it only disappeared into a void.

This was a difficult year, and it was the year you claimed who you were. Do you remember that? You claimed why you show up and it was never for gratitude or to be celebrated. You claimed building a liberatory world regardless of anyone else. You claimed a liberatory life instead of the liberatory death you yearned for at the time, knowing that sitting with the hard work is what breaks cycles of despair.

So much happened after, and I wish I could say it immediately got better—it didn't, but the work you did made it doable. Every day you believed in collective liberation, every day you believed that a better world was guaranteed, that living liberated lives did not need to wait for a world without systems of oppression. Every day you were right. Utopia is to be lived every day, and it was the work you did that allows me to step into my role every day now.

Many were skeptical of this approach—to be honest, as I have aged and I look back at memories, I wonder how I wasn't skeptical myself. I know you were frustrated at times, but you honored that frustration and still showed up, and even knowing the world that I know I don't know if I would have shown up like you did.

The work you and countless others did to support people to show up as themselves in a liberated world meant that as state violence increased communities had more support. Little by little, our dependencies on the state shifted. Communities built housing structures, offered medical and mental health support pathways, fed one another, were accountable together, grew together.

The world changed after. Fascism made itself undeniable for some time and the planet changed its rhythms through floods, fires, and earthquakes that we started feeling everywhere. The bird flu and other pandemics changed how we cared for one another even more. So many knew how to be together and how to support one another in the process due to the hundreds of years of work so many did. The skill you developed and worldbuilding you and so many others did throughout your life. Then it happened and then the work continued after and here I am now.

I make that sound quick and easy—it wasn't, there was despair, hopelessness, and I still remember the loneliness gnawing at your being and knowing that so many felt the same way. But it was also filled with joy, love, hope, spirituality, and growth. Laughter echoes in my mind as I remember fires, loss of so much life, that there didn't seem room to breathe, let alone grieve. And yet, I remember us being held, literally and figuratively, and fighting for something that mattered so much that dying was not of concern but our yearning for liberation so great not for ourselves but for everyone who came after. I remember laughter. I remember you shining so brightly throughout.

***

I write this over a decade into liberation. My thirties are a distant past, barely remembered by my bones that are preoccupied with their own existence. I remember, as we were about to turn thirty, realizing that my age is still a factor,

Dear Yaffa (as you await liberation) 19

even for someone who had been disabled their entire life. The effects of age compound the impact of disability, and there is no running from it, though I have learned to enjoy every ache as a sign of liberation.

I think about this memory as I write this because I remember the devastation that followed your solar return. I remember trying to balance disability with responsibility for a liberated world. I remember you speaking again and again about the movement spaces that were mass disabling events. I remember wanting to give up but knowing that our survival was tied to liberation; giving up on liberation meant death, and although we would welcome death with open arms like a long-lost friend, that exchange did not make sense.

So many would be wondering what exactly happened, when, where, how, and who ultimately led us to liberation. I am amazed at your sense of purpose and belief that liberation would happen regardless and the answers to those questions did not matter. They didn't and they still don't. There are thousands of stories from those years, thousands of events, hundreds of thousands of actions, hundreds of riots and although we claim there was a revolution, the reality is that the revolution existed in the land and in rural communities before it ever made it to the metropoles where it made the news. Then there were no more regular news broadcasts or newspapers, independent reporters on the frontlines of genocides were the only ones doing reporting and finding ways to disseminate their accounts through independent journalism networks. News spread like wildfire through communities. Then the 'big ones' happened. Istanbul fell, triggering a mass reaction in the Arab world and they finally rose up against Zionism, with arms, ideas, and world opinion on their side,

20   *Letters from a Living Utopia*

prioritizing liberation over self-preservation. Cuba fell after years of embargo and Yankee imperialism, and then rose again, like Puerto Rico when students, teachers, farmers all revolted against the banking and debt systems that sought to recolonize them for years. Los Angeles, El Paso, CDMX, Hawaii, Asheville, Denver, followed by New York, all subsumed by wildfire or flood. San Francisco and Boston were late but followed along, popular power rising out of catastrophe many times and in many places. Many still remember the teta uprisings. Many remember the sex workers, drag queens, and dolls lighting New York City on fire. Many remember when Heathrow was completely occupied, followed by Newark, Dallas, and Charlotte. I wasn't as involved with the revolutions in North Asia, the Caribbean, and throughout Africa, but they were the blueprints and we circulated news and analysis constantly. Everyday became a new blueprint. But I have never thought of liberation work as when, what, why, how, who. To try to answer those questions is to reduce revolutions to single events, but they're not. They are far more beautiful in their complexity. To try to answer *who* is meaningless without offering witness to all the dead, the ones left behind, those who moved forward, and those who never made it to today.

I honor them all, I honor us all, I honor you all, but I do not send back the expectations of the events of my world based on my own experience of them—for I was not everywhere, no one was. To tell you how it began is to assume I was there when it did, as if this wasn't a process for 550 years. To tell you who was there is to know every name, something we can never hold. Answers are a responsibility, and even

Dear Yaffa (as you await liberation) 21

if I was able to give you an exact timeline and step-by-step process, that wouldn't change a single thing. You know this, like I have known this—liberation is not a single person's job or the profession of a few chosen people. You can carry every answer, but it means nothing if you are alone.

At thirty-two, you mostly were alone, even as thousands of people read your work and you spoke in front of hundreds of thousands. A lot of people were alone—by design—and that was part of the problem. A lot of you knew what to do, a lot of you knew how to dismantle systems and ways of building beyond them—but you were alone or in small groups. It wasn't answers we searched for—it was commitment and a responsibility to collective liberation.

I write to you liberated, with everyone around me liberated, on land that is liberated under stars that can rest without the threat of another genocidal civilization's occupation. That may provide solace to some back then, but what I wanted to know more than anything else when I was you was not whether or not we would be liberated and not even whether or not we would die. I wanted to know what a world that fights for life looked and felt like.

Death is guaranteed. Disability is guaranteed. Liberation is guaranteed. These things do not exist for the satisfaction of oppressive systems, yet it was hard to picture them outside the oppressive gaze.

It was in 2025 when you almost let go of the fire for a liberated world. Living with colonial oppression eats away at your soul, I know this, you knew this. You understood that the world you lived in fed off of labor of the living and the bones of the dead. You understood that the line between the

22   *Letters from a Living Utopia*

violence of settler nation states and the violence sitting on top of and throughout our communities was blurry, and the forms of control imposed on you were fascist whether named or unnamed. This was the year you pushed hard against the culture of opportunism, reward, and accumulation that suffocated the air in social justice communities, claiming that you have never done this labor for gratitude or appreciation because you have mostly only known the risks and the threats that come from real liberation work. This was the year that you felt so loved as an individual and tried explaining to loved ones and communities that you are not an individual and so cannot feel love when you're separated from your ecosystem.

There is a lot I don't remember all these years later, but 2025 is a year I remember between the haze and the ever-changing currents of liberatory work as the oil of fascism threatened to become the entire current.

Remember nearly drowning in 2022? On the abandoned Puerto Rico beach where the current asked to swallow you whole? It is fear that increases the risk of drowning, our lungs naturally built to float in water. You knew this, like I do now, but for a moment you were scared, the only time you've ever been scared of the water. The water was home and still is, but in that moment all knowledge was gone, disappeared by the fire.

It was a moment and then you remembered that you are of the water; if the water takes your body, let it be a gift and let us be generous and grateful. Instead of fighting against it, you allowed the current to pull you and as it relented you shifted, finding your way back to the white pearly sand beach. As the fear of a fascist world rose so did the fear of our liberation,

Dear Yaffa (as you await liberation) 23

and many could no longer differentiate between the currents of liberation and the oil spills threatening to claim them.

Fear is natural, it is human. Fear is a motivator, in the waters that nearly claimed your fear was a question of life and death, a question of worthiness of struggle. Fear is a question in a moment in time that demands an answer, and indeed, there are consequences when we do not provide an answer. To be afraid without working toward an answer is to freeze in water, making it easier to claim you. And when attempting to save others from drowning, their panic can often take you down with them.

That's what 2025 felt like: so many drowning in the waters of fascism, not realizing that in their fear response they pulled others deeper with them. Many did not even notice as they were drowning.

You noticed. You noticed. You noticed.

And you remembered that you have the training to do liberatory work amidst so many drowning, to support those closest as you found ways to mobilize others to plunge in and join the rescue mission. I remember us sitting with a friend and realizing, "If this was a few years ago I would be concerned about martyring myself, but I know how to move in this, I have had to."

You were remembering how years of learning helped you understand that burnout is not primarily due to overwork and pushing yourself beyond your capacity, but more often, burnout happens when there is value misalignment in our labor and who we are. I still remember what I learned from you to this very day, that the foundation we build our work on is important. If we are taught that we will always be celebrated for doing "the right thing" then the work becomes ego driven and when we are not celebrated our capacity for doing "the right thing" is diminished and at times extinguished.

Liberation work is deeply generational, rooted in the basis of what makes us human, a deep love that extends far beyond the interpersonal into the deepest crevices of a universe we will never know. Liberation is rooted in land, in spirit, in stardust—built into the foundation of the very first human and everything beyond.

By that point you had gone through cycle after cycle of burnout and it was always resistance and dehumanization that burned you out. You knew then that burnout is like an engine that is leaking fuel, and you realized how healing can feel like a self-sustaining engine.

You knew that moving toward utopia is moving toward wholeness. But that wasn't always reflected in the communities around you as they also grasped with their own lives and yearnings for liberation. We are meant to be collectivist and liberatory as a species, but even the most collectivist of species can learn individualism within a single lifetime. And they can also be liberated within a single lifetime.

I know you're not wondering if I am liberated as an individual—I know that. I know that you care about the "I" that exists within community, the "I" that is never a single body. I am liberated, the entirety of my ecosystem. And you were right: we only got here by living it and those who didn't came along anyways when crises marred everything they had ever known. Liberation is guaranteed.

I am grateful for the learning that you had done, and today as I sit with my aching body, I am grateful for the thing that allowed you to continue the work. It was something you

Dear Yaffa (as you await liberation) 25

had learned again and again, tapped into Indigenous Palestinian and Islamic culture to enforce, then learned it again through your spiritual practice of yoga. It was the learning that changed burnout forever and made it irrelevant.

On your first day of yoga teacher training, you were told that mastering asanas is what allows you to begin yoga. You had known this about prayer prior but worded that way allowed it to click. Our bodies are brilliant and capable of so much, but they, like everything else, must practice to be able to extend their limits. As your brain snapped yet again and you were no longer able to process time and space you were reminded of this, having lost the practice. Our bodies must be at a certain level of training to be able to carry the work of liberation, otherwise they are overloaded and unable to proceed. Properly training our bodies allows us to carry everything. You learned this when you could no longer breathe and you were in need of surgery. You learned the difference between lungs that can hold and lungs that cannot. You learned that everything is connected and you remembered. You remembered that, yes, burnout is primarily about the foundation we have and the conflicting values around us, but it is also about training our bodies to hold that. The weight of liberation is heavy, and it takes a lifetime of training for our bodies to be able to carry it all. Thankfully, enough people learned this and carried it together and lived it together, and slowly their own limits were expanded.

You knew this then as I know this now: that even if liberation had happened in 2025 there weren't enough who knew how to live it. So we waited a little longer. I send you love and patience as you wait, the type of wait that is filled with work. I send love and patience as a form of gratitude to everything

I learned from you along the way and in response to a letter you wrote me in 2024 sending me love and patience. I am back at the Black Mountains one final time, my final trip to Abya Yala, your letter my greatest treasure.

> *I sit on a clearing in the Black Mountains at the end of a naked yoga retreat writing this. The sun on my skin, nourishing every part of me. The ocean extends in the distance, past downward hills and forests, birds chirping and others flying through the image as if automated.*
>
> *I yearn to build you this peace and calm every day. The world—my world is not yet liberated, but for you I already feel liberated. I will leave this mountain today, I will fight for everyone's liberation as I depart and someday you and I will see each other across a mirror, you will not fully know who I am or that I sent you these words but you will know because you will be doing the same for another, just like the child did for me, just like countless ancestors before—sending almost identical messages across the ages. Hope emitted into the universe and recycled until the last living being.*

I love you, in the past, the present, and the future,
Yaffa

LETTER TWO
17/Leo/6

Dear Suleiman,

This evening, you asked me about where I come from, the question springing to your three-year-old mind as I read one of your favorite books before bedtime.

I was awestruck by the question, although I should have expected it, and instead of answering in detail, I smiled and said I come from where all our people have come from. I come from the land and to the land I will return.

I've now put you in bed and found my way to my desk overlooking the garden and sheep fields, the Mediterranean waves a lull in the background, all of it too dark to see except for the stray sheep stirring in the night.

28   *Letters from a Living Utopia*

I write this letter to you for a later time when this answer will make sense. Tonight, your brilliant and curious mind is too young to understand that "Where do you come from?" was a deeply painful question in the world I come from.

What I did not say, and I hope to convey now, is that it is not *where* I come from, but rather *when* I come from that complicates matters. For the where has always been known, but in the world I grew up in, I was not permitted to say Falasteen or Canaan without being targeted and attacked, actions that are incomprehensible today. In that world, to say I am from the land did not mean what it means today. In fact, it meant very little and was usually weaponized by people determined to colonize us and steal our land.

I grew up at a time when to be Falasteeni was to be where genocide and displacement intersect, concepts you have not yet learned about. I grew up in what we would have called the diaspora, separate from home.

Where I come from, the diaspora was the norm for many of us, born and grown away from home, most forced, some by choice, and some—like myself—barred from ever returning home. It was over seventy-six years after my family's displacement that I finally stepped on Falasteeni land.

Those of us in diaspora were also not the same. Some were able to leave home with resources and take root in other occupied lands. Some were displaced with nothing at all but were still able to root, while others still could never root.

I am of the latter group.

Before I turned thirty, I had lived in ten of what we used to call "nation-states," displaced from one to the other—an immigrant, a refugee, an undocumented person, someone

Dear Suleiman 29

with various other statuses in between (all things that I hope you never witness or experience).

Where I come from is a place where childhood friends exist a year at a time, where the physical places I lived in outnumber the years of my life.

Where I come from is not a place, it is a scattered history of oppression shaping and constraining identities that thankfully have no relevance today but back then created a partition that reinforced a hierarchy of value, of whose lives and homes mattered.

I honor that you are capable of witnessing this place without attaching to it, and I do not share this letter with you to ground us only in the place I am from. I write this to tell you that the blood flowing within you and within me was detoured from our home, and blood does not forget. I pray that I have allowed our blood to heal in all the ways it needed to return home. I want to prepare you in case it has not fully healed, in case it yearns for healing now that my home is yours.

You see, where I am from is also where you come from, not physically but rather spiritually. You come from the best parts of this time. Your other caretakers will share their own stories with you along the way, as I share parts of mine here.

Life *when* I am from was different. The years after my thirtieth birthday, nearly four decades ago, my world witnessed genocides in a way that they had never witnessed before, and I hope will never again. Just an hour south by train was the first of what would be known as the most visible genocides of the *when* I am from, in Gaza. I was thousands of miles away as family I barely knew were killed, as every person I worked with was killed again and again, a cycle of constantly losing everyone, not able to return home to die with them. This was over a decade into my own liberation- and utopia-oriented organizing and mobilizing across various continents. With every new genocide, war, famine, flood, drought, and wildfire, I tried to organize new pathways for community care.

You see, *where* I come from, community care was not the norm, but being poor (you might have many questions about this absurd concept), it was a matter of survival, and I made sure it was the norm in *my* world. Being Falasteeni, displaced for the third time by the time I was born, meant we had to take care of each other during and after the catastrophe and across every border and separation, whether checkpoint, cage, or country.

The story I read to you this evening was about a child who asked, "Who am I?" and "Where do I come from?" They wondered if they come from the sun or moon or stars or the ocean or the mountains or olive trees. They wondered if they are a tree yearning for the sun, or a whale so deep in the ocean the sun is worlds away. They wondered if they were like a seed in the ground, reliant on the sun but never seeing it. They wondered if they were stalagmites in a cave, never knowing what exists outside. What we didn't get to this evening, that I hope we'll finish tomorrow, is that they discover they are of it all. They are of the sun and moon, of trees and mountains and oceans, they are both hidden like the seed and stalagmites and regal and visible like a hawk swooping through the sky. They learn they are a little of everything, for they are human.

Dear Suleiman 31

In my world, things were different. Every human was divided into "nationalities" that forced the question of *who I am* into the question of *where I come from*. Dozens more questions lived between those two and they also created structures for limiting possibilities. We were not human, we were identities, and if we were the seed then we were told and conditioned to believe that we could not be the fruit, our destiny denied.

Most struggled to answer the question *who am I?* Now, to say I am of the land is to be able to access community, home, resources, all kinds of things that we were stripped of at the time. It's perhaps better to use the word "robbed" here instead because that's all it was: theft. We had enough of everything, even more than we do now, but we were robbed.

I share all of this so you have deeper wisdom about those of us caring for you today, those who were raised and conditioned in a world different than yours. And within that world we found one another and cared for one another. We were all trying to build a world where everyone can be born, live, and die cared for. We took care of one another across thousands of miles, many of us never knowing how we were impacting one another.

It was care that gave me the answer to who I am in the world that I am from. I had experienced community care as a child; it was the only way my family could have survived war and displacement. Back then I thought this was normal, that everyone supported others and received support, building community every step of the way. I was wrong. Many people at the time did not need to care for others to survive, benefiting from resources stolen from others. Many never learned reciprocity or community because their lives were anathema to it.

As I grew older, staying rooted and determined in this work regardless of how the reward economy at the time tried to bribe me into forgetting myself and my purpose, I thought that everyone who grew up with community care would continue that tradition, not realizing that many accepted the bribe of assimilation. My own family forgot, and it would take them decades to remember.

It was a lonely time in a lot of ways. To care was to be punished, and nation-states made it illegal to decommodify the things people need to live and to redistribute resources, while communities were conditioned to compete with one another, operating from the same cages of identity that the nation-states policed with their borders.

I built community care anyways. I always have, and into my old age, I know I always will. By the time you read this, it will make sense to you. I might have passed, but you'll have grown up seeing the work I do in community, and you will remember me by it. You will have memories of me talking endlessly about life and death, healing through the land and spirit, leading meditations and artistic spaces channeling the voice of the universe that lives within each of us. It might seem natural to you since you see it everywhere around you.

I laugh writing this because that may not have been what you expected with everything I said about the when and where I was born. Sure, there were consequences to doing all this work, but so what? I am human, of the land and sea, of spirit and a consciousness I can barely begin to understand. The colonizers of the old world restricted us because they knew our power, and some of us did it anyways.

Dear Suleiman 33

This work is still ongoing even today, long into a liberated world. I listened then as I listen now. I breathed with others like I breathe now. I share stories through writing and verbal storytelling now like I did then. Back then, this spirit work was tied to the work we did to move stolen resources back into communities they were stolen from. We supported people so they could survive the systems of oppression that stole everything from them, something we no longer have to do. But you inherit a world full of the same tools, the same practices we used to liberate ourselves.

Of course, now I get to spend more time with loved ones, caring for others in more permanent ways, and I get to talk about goats more often. But as I think about it, I have always been talking about goats. Someday, I'll tell you the story of my first theater play, *harvesting olives*; I mentioned goats then too.

I am no longer lonely in this work. Instead of a few being responsible for living liberation now everyone is responsible for liberated living. I hope you and everyone who comes after you never forget to live with this freedom.

I come from the place where community care built me— and built you. I come from the intersection of a world dying and a world rebuilding itself anew. I come from peace as genocide unfolded around me, as bombs dropped from the sky in front of me. I come from a home before it was ground beneath my feet.

Now, I come from a place where I get to be in your world and in many other peoples' world. You were born in the best of every aspect of that community, surrounded by loved ones capable of witnessing you.

34   *Letters from a Living Utopia*

I still remember your first question to me, you asked who I was. I was so proud of my response then as I am now. I am of spirit, and I have many roles in this life, one of which includes caring for you. I am of the ecosystem that birthed me and the ecosystem I die in. You didn't understand any of these words and were distracted by then, but I hope that I get to live up to these words, for you, for me, and for us all.

Yaffa

LETTER THREE
28/Virgo/7

Dear Dana,

Do you remember when you called me and said, "I have an article I want you to publish, it's already in your inbox"? Well, I do. I dropped everything and looked at my inbox to find an article titled "The Monstrosity of Men." It's not every day that I received articles like that, let alone from my twelve-year-old sister. The article needed fewer edits than any other submission I'd received, and within hours it was published.

This happened a couple of years after another memorable incident where you sat the family down and told us you no longer wanted us to ask you "how are you?" You said it was a waste of time, a stand-in question enroute to the actual question we wanted to ask and why couldn't we just skip the filler and go right to the question.

Remember how the revolution came and went and it was as if nothing had really changed for you? You were the first person that seemed self-actualized to me, even as a child. You knew what you were about, what you wanted your life to be and look like, and were comfortable enough to claim it in a way that I rarely saw back then—and even now, it is an achievement.

Mama used to think that you learned from me, and I suppose you did, but I learned from you by living my life in a way that you could witness. The cycle of growth is beautiful to me, a never-ending spiral that lives beyond all of us, none of us knowing where it begins or ends.

You taught me to claim everything that I am, and I hope in turn I supported you in claiming all that you are—although as a Capricorn you hardly needed me or anyone at all.

In the first few decades of life, I had witnessed countless individuals waiting for the fall of oppression to feel liberated. I also witnessed countless individuals not *feeling* liberated when we did move into a liberated world, after the last nation-state was put to rest, a return to Indigenous sovereignty. I have also witnessed that those who chose to claim liberation as the world was being remade were the ones who knew how to exist in a fully liberated world. We can work with others as they find their way to liberation, but, ultimately, they must claim it.

You knew then, as so many more know now, that liberation has always been about being everything that we are meant to be. The old systems of oppression taught us that we wouldn't be everything we're meant to be, that we had to exist within the confines of a world built by their profit and their

Dear Dana 37

domination, a system that used racial patriarchal colonial rule for over five hundred years to denigrate both humanity and the whole living world. We have always been liberated, what we claimed along the way is dismantling the systems that created the barriers to being everything that we are. And just like you claimed yourself in how you were spoken to all those years ago, so many found ways to claim their own liberation and used that as a foundation to dismantle the systems and build this world.

I am writing to you now because I miss you despite seeing you just a few moments ago. I miss the years lost between us that we never experienced together.

I watched you walk into your being every day, and you reinspired me again and again. I'm not quite sure how we got here. It feels like just yesterday that you were in my arms in the middle of the night, just hours after you were born. Later still, you were in my arms as you cried from a fever, tears, pee, and poop all rushing out to greet me as I tried to soothe you. Even back then, you were self-conscious and ashamed.

I watched you crawl around, a filled diaper following you in the middle of the night because we were the only ones awake.

Then I left when I was around seventeen. You were four.

The worst part of living on the streets was not being there for your first day of school, your second, your third . . .

I watched you grow from a distance, missing every day beyond the few that I visited.

You were seven when I wrote to you for your eighteenth birthday to explain why I was no longer there. I never gave you that letter.

38 *Letters from a Living Utopia*

I blinked and you were ten, putting people on alert, saying no one should ask you how you are; rather, they should ask you what they really want to know.

I blinked and you were twelve, asking me to publish an article for you about the monstrosity of men.

I blinked again and you were eighteen.

I moved closer, the revolution began and, in ways we felt but did not understand, ended. We were home, finally, and I still honor the lessons I learned from you all these years later.

I don't share this easily, but it's important for you to know that you were one of the few who inspired me to live. In my world, dying was easier than living, as I drifted away from you and everyone else.

You don't know this, and I always hoped you only find out when you were ready to claim this knowledge and release it in the ways that fed your soul: I wrote over a dozen suicide notes a few months after my twentieth birthday. The first and last were to you. They were to you because I was conscious of how we all fit into each other's lives. Every pain is felt by everyone, every success the same. Dying at twenty would have meant a different world, just like you not claiming yourself would have created a different world. Instead, I claimed my life little by little as you claimed everything you are.

You were a part of my understanding and my claiming purpose. Every action we take serves a purpose. Strategy is understanding that purpose and working to practice that purpose with community. Death and life can both be strategic, but it was a long time until I fully understood that we are meant to live liberated lives always.

May you always be all that you are,
Yaffa

LETTER FOUR
20/Sagittarius/4

Dear Liberation,

I write to you today because during a recent conversation with a community member we were reflecting on the love we carry for you, especially in a world where we experience you with ease and do not have to fight for you in the same way as we had in our younger years. We both decided to write to you and share our journeys with one another.

You did not happen overnight, but it was still strange to wake up one day and realize that you were here. The work didn't end then, but the sun rose, and we had a new beginning.

40   *Letters from a Living Utopia*

I do not have an accurate count for how many I lost; how many were lost collectively. Those numbers would overwhelm me, but I remind myself that we lost far more without fighting for you at all.

I remember for years saying that liberation was going to happen, that living utopia is possible every single day. I have always known that my people will be free, that our land will be free. The world was always going to be liberated. It was always a matter of time.

With that knowledge in the back of my mind, the question that arose from an early age was what role I would be playing as we moved toward a liberated world.

As a child, in Jummah prayer, I would envision myself becoming a giant robot capable of destroying army bases. Then, around the age of eight, I found out about the Mahdi, the Muslim savior who would liberate the world.

Throughout my childhood, I saw how everyone carried the torch of liberation differently. Some through radical actions, some through community care, some through kindness, some through relationships, some through hope.

I have always been drawn to the power of culture workers, those who can name and represent living utopia in the now as well as the portal to an inevitable liberated world. Those who help others cradle hope.

Hope is transformative, a guiding force going beyond what is ordinarily seen as possible. Without hope, our lives stagnate—we lose purpose and momentum. Hope is so powerful that it can be shared and held collectively by a community even when it's lost on an individual level.

In my training as a Certified Peer Support Specialist, we'd often say a core part of our role is to hold hope for people.

Dear Liberation 41

Especially when they are not able to hold it for themselves, we accompany them on their journeys for self-actualization. Holding hope collectively allows us to give ourselves and others grace in liberation.

But why then can one be accused of being naive for hoping? Why does hope become so destructive at times? How can hope be weaponized into cynicism?

Waiting for liberation, carrying hope can feel devastating.

I remember at an event over thirty years ago on Šikaae konki (in what had been known as Chicago), a participant asked me if talking about utopia risks pushing people away from movements because it seems impossible to hope for utopia. I responded at the time that the devastation that comes from not attaining liberation is due to attached hope instead of nonattached hope.

When we associate hope with an outcome, we are often devastated in our practice. Why continue to work for something that is not happening? This leads us into a cycle of hope, devastation, helplessness, depression, and then hope again. It is not lost on me that, in English, the root of the word *hope* is the same root as for the word *desperation*. When we believe we control outcomes then we desperately hold onto hope because if we do not receive the desired outcome we will be devastated.

For years I witnessed that devastation, again and again, so much so that as I grew into adulthood, liberation was synonymous with it. Moving toward liberation was pain (not in a good way). It was the pain that felt stuck, that festered and became infected, and it usually led to amputation with people leaving and never coming back. But still, I had to hold onto a vision of liberation work that was actually about joy.

42   *Letters from a Living Utopia*

Not everyone moved toward this before the world was liberated. Even as the world was remade, some could not feel joy when they thought of utopia, instead their veins constricted in uneager anticipation for the conversations and actions around transformation.

Today, I would add to that answer that hoping for liberation is an extension of our own liberation. Liberation is not given, nor can it be taken away—it is simply human. A caged bird is still a bird, and the cage is a cage. Systems of oppression were systems of oppression, and we have always been human. Claiming ourselves even with the existence of systems of oppression allows us to see the cage for what it is, a rusty, fragile creation that can never be anything more than temporary.

I reflect on this today, because I am witnessing the fear of a return to systemic oppression permeating around me. Fear of systemic oppression is natural and is needed, a reminder to always show up fully in the ways we are meant to. Fear built on a reality that systemic oppression is inevitable can become destructive. This fear has existed pre-liberation and will exist throughout it. What we do with that fear has always been the assignment. A fear that makes us believe something that isn't true without space to move through it is what was weaponized to create the systems of oppression we fought against.

We must, back then and today, build our communities' foundation to be able to hold and sustain hope for liberation always, the liberation that is guaranteed, not the liberation that is a temporary relief from systems of oppression. This work requires a lifelong journey developing an understanding and recognition that our bodies, minds, and spirits have to be *trained* to carry and witness hope.

Dear Liberation 43

I inhale from the lit sage nearby as I write this, allowing it to fill my lungs. Our lungs carry grief. When processed, grief turns to hope. Therefore, there is no hope without grief. To try to carry a weight that is too heavy is to fall underneath that weight, to be devastated, to break down. Without training our lungs we do not know how to carry either. I trained to be able to witness and carry through daily swimming, prayer, memorizing liberatory texts, yoga, meditation, journaling, writing, and dabke. I train my body, my mind, and my spirit. I have supported others to do the same.

***

I feel I have to apologize to you on behalf of the people of my world, for too many of us did not take your weight seriously and fell apart underneath it. It speaks volumes to how we were conditioned away from our responsibility to find you and how little we truly knew about you.

The truth, though, is that no one person can carry the weight of liberation, there is no amount of training that will allow a single person to carry this weight—both the grief and the hope of liberation. None of this is or was ever meant to be done alone.

This weight is meant to be carried by many, grounded in the land and amplified by spirit. I can train all I want but there is no carrying this alone. I know, I have broken under this weight before, until I understood that I cannot carry this alone and what I carry matters.

In my lifetime, I went from living in a world where hope was to be held close to my heart because it was seen as naive, to a world where lack of hope seemed violent, to nonattached hope, and finally to the world of today—a place where liberation is in our every breath.

Nonattachment began for me in the form of *Insha'Allah*—if Allah wills it. In the household I grew up in, it was a promise and a prayer. A promise to do all you can to do what you set to do. A prayer asking for what is for the best. Finally, it was a release of any attachment to the outcome, for if it was not meant to be it would not be.

Insha'Allah was also about hope, as is all prayer. The hope that lives in Insha'Allah is nonattached hope, hope that is not defined through success and failure because it is always for the best—even when we do not understand the best.

Hope is nonattached. We control our actions, our reactions, but the outcomes are beyond us.

We did not know when Falasteen would be free, when the peoples and the lands of Sudan, Turtle Island, the Congo, Haiti, Armenia, Kashmir, etc., would find their freedom, but it was always going to happen. We did not take action in those many moments before liberation because we knew *those actions* would free us. We acted because it is the right thing to do and because liberation is ours. But we knew we would be free, and that outcome was not ours alone.

Hope is recognizing that we get to be a part of the labor of something that is not ours to control. What happens will happen, but determining outcomes is beyond my soul grade.

Today, in this liberated world, the barriers that would have prevented others from showing up as their full selves are no longer present. I am still a spirit healer, but I do not carry anything beyond hope for anyone in my community. What happens beyond our shared space is beyond me. Whether or

Dear Liberation 45

not we share space is beyond me. And I'm no longer alone, there are countless other healers with different modalities and shared modalities, and everyone is invested in one another's continued liberation.

Even now, decades later, I support community in healing from capitalism but now we have the resources we need, we have our connection to land and to one another, connection to the universe beyond us and we move through it without the consequences of capitalism, without the dread and anticipation of the violence that is to come.

Our practice now is to reroute our neuropathways so we may wholeheartedly accept the job of liberation. Our brain has billions of neuropathways and, over time, creates shortcuts to ease immensely complex reactions. These shortcuts are why we immediately react to various stimuli without our control. These shortcuts allow us to do the incredibly complex, amazing things we do every day and at times, are the reason we respond the way we do to "pain," "triggers," etc. I put quotations around pain and triggers because they are not universally defined and understood, and they exist in both an oppressive world and a liberated one.

Pain, triggers, and all other concepts are also what we make them to be, especially when they are not grounded in their own roots. Everything and anything can be reframed. The reaction is what matters. The key is to change the neurological response entirely. It is not enough for this work to elicit a neutral response; it must be a response filled with ease and with joy. Ideally, dreaming, thinking, imagining—anything at all—of utopia would elicit a calming and easing effect. Otherwise, our state of being as we approach utopia will be one of weariness, exhaustion, and repulsion. We would carry the same emotions we have living in an oppressive society, routing us away from utopia.

When difficult conversations are joyful and immensely hopeful, and not simply something painful that must be avoided, we begin our inner transformation for utopia. The first step is realizing that this is possible in the first place, and then we claim nonattached hope.

We can fill conversations around utopia with joy and allow ourselves to be at ease moving through them. I am fortunate to be able to build spaces that cultivate joy and facilitate conversations in a way that feeds our souls instead of drains our energy.

***

I write this from a place of gratitude for you, liberation. You are not just an outcome or destination, you have always been a way of life for me, and a pathway for immense joy.

It took a while; slowly, over the first decades of my life, joy became inseparable from utopia-building, and that was when I could truly begin to envision utopia.

I am grateful for that gift, of you now, you then, you always. May every soul find you again and again.

With gratitude,
Yaffa

LETTER FIVE
5/Aries/12

Dear Reem,

Waking up this morning, I found myself remembering our conversation in Bethlehem City Hostel, two days after entering Falasteen for the very first time—my very first time. It was my thirty-second birthday. Over tea, we talked about nonattachment in relationships, astrological yearnings, and again and again, the conversation returned to wanting to live in a liberated Falasteen. A free Falasteen was *how* we wanted to live.

I smile now, remembering how dreams come true.

My time with you reminded me and currently reminds me of how utopia is lived, not just dreamed and imagined. On occupied land, our occupied land, we weren't talking about liberating the land, we spoke about liberating our bodies, our minds, our relationships, our relationship to sex, everything.

In the midst of a genocide, on a land we had been barred from our entire lives, on the eve of the largest escalation in the war yet, we spoke of love and nonattachment.

Love, sex, and intimacy were all things I grew up afraid of, because although I had countless examples of community care, liberatory practice, and visions of justice throughout my childhood, I did not have much in the realm of love. Sure, growing up, my community was caring and often kind and definitely resilient, but I would not claim that it was a loving community.

Though there was community, friendship, and family, love was often weaponized and shrouded in control. So many of us were robbed of the freedom that love brings on the path of survival. Love was considered care to support our survival, very little existed beyond it between wars and a post-9/11 childhood. Love was irrelevant in the face of survival, something I carried with me, and as I entered my thirties, I understood that there was no room for love that didn't fit within my collective liberation work.

Because I had believed it for years, it took me a while to understand that no matter what the form of love—whether friendship, intimate, sexual, community, or any other—I can't control it. I thought I had to be in a specific kind of relationship and it had to look a certain way, or it wasn't real or allowed.

Dear Reem 49

That morning, after praying together, we spoke of non-attached love, and I learned that there is no such thing as attached love. Love is nonattached, or it is corrupted.

I send a prayer in remembrance of bell hooks, grateful that we existed at the same time on this planet and for her teachings about love, which supported my healing journey toward an understanding and practice of revolutionary love.

This was a decades-long journey prior to our being together in Falasteen, to move away from what I would later think of as puritanical relationship culture, and to find its antithesis in a safe, loving, and revolutionary queer culture. We realigned ourselves to value the full spectrum of our bodies and our desires, not policed by binary classifications like pure and dirty, creating ethical polyamory out of the property logics of monogamy, celebrating the sensuality and eroticism of sex. We yearned to create endless nonattached relationships, finding love not in bounded and bordered relationships but in all the ways we invested in each other, even those we will never meet.

I am remembering our conversation, and although I brought most of this forward, my learning of love would not be complete without you.

Within nonattachment, we do not control and we are not controlled, but this does not erase the exercise in choice. In fact, it amplifies it. When we choose *how* to love, we can find freedom within nonattachment.

Remember our conversation about how love elevates? Love is meant to be liberatory and moves us toward all that we are meant to be. Love is a source of abundance in our lives. To love is to be elevated, it is to grow. If I am to love someone, then I must access parts of myself that are beyond my capabilities. Love is not just about doing what I know and I'm comfortable with, it is about growing to meet another along the way. We are each unique, no matter the similarities, so it makes sense that loving is not just what we know, there is always an extension beyond, which ultimately serves as a bridge for essential growth in our lives. We are always meant to be growing.

If I arrive every day with the purpose of nurturing my own growth what would that look like? What does it look like to show up with the purpose of nurturing another's growth? The answer is love.

You asked, "What is growth?" To me, growth is interconnected with spirituality because it is through connection that we grow.

Spirituality is connection. In the absence of spiritual connection, the path will always be toward individualism and separation.

We had witnessed this phenomenon at the start of the COVID-19 pandemic in 2020 and with the Palestinian liberation movement in fall 2023, when more and more communities were having conversations about individualism and collectivism. It is in these moments that many were able to move toward building a culture of care with one another, realizing that there is only separation without collectivism.

Systems of oppression are inherently anti-spiritual. Secular and religious institutions play a role in maintaining these systems of oppression, which have hijacked spiritual practices that predate their existence. We learned throughout the twentieth and twenty-first centuries that both were vulnerable to

Dear Reem 51

being captured by fascism. A return to spirit is resistance to these institutions, it is the acknowledgment that spirituality cannot be confined within state, colonial, or capitalist institutions or systems. Spirituality can never be confined.

Proclaiming to love is not the same as loving. Love is a verb, it is not a feeling or a sensation, it is an action, a practice, a tool of connection that shapes our reality. Is the reality we experience together loving or is it not? If not, then there are actions to be taken to move us toward loving. I revel in the magic we feel these days, as we've built a world where we can honor fullness and the expansion of interconnected life. We have the love we need to move through our actions, to develop them, hone them, be in them, then grow some more.

Today, we thrive with this understanding, whereas before, we built it with the hope that utopia would someday unfold around us, protecting us and propelling us as systems of oppression fell around us.

I'm in the community center in Yaffa, Falasteen as I write this. Children are engaged in every kind of conversation imaginable. They are comfortable, something I did not know was possible at their age. Do you remember the Baladna Youth Center in El-Nasra? Do you remember how the kids surrounded us in their comfort and we were both so overwhelmed? Here they were, in an area so targeted in the midst of an escalation toward a war that sought to annihilate them and yet so natural in their existence.

Natural. Natural. Natural. The word natural had been so weaponized against so many of us within imperialist white supremacist empires. Natural became white. Natural was slavery, all kinds of genocide, endless forms of oppression.

52   *Letters from a Living Utopia*

Natural became eugenics. Tears trail my cheeks as I write this, springing from reservoirs of my existence where pain is still stored.

Maya sits next to me, not making eye contact until I do so. I smile and nod and they smile back. We don't say anything, I keep writing, their presence supporting me to finish this letter to you.

Maya allows me to reflect on how love is not simply a personal and interpersonal practice. Love is a foundation for community building, and it operates on every plane of our existence. If we took this definition into our relationship with ourselves, others, and into every aspect of our lives, who would we be and what would our lives look like?

I ask these questions because I feel our conversations then—moving to Al-Aqsa, then Haifa, as we were told to shelter for four days amidst the escalation of war—were questions asked and not answered, because we weren't able to live the moments beyond the questions.

You hated your job then—do you remember that? I remember us sitting at a restaurant overlooking the hills of Al-Quds, watching the sunset. You perked up, asking, "What if?"

That single spark of your imagination and every question you asked yourself after supported rebuilding dozens of houses that the Zionist apartheid state had demolished. That moment helped shift our political work together in a way that no one but the three of us sitting there will ever know. That spark was nonattached love, and I have watched you for years bring that to the forefront of everything you do. You never again said you hated your job after that day, though we were still desperately surviving capitalism and building a

Dear Reem 53

world beyond it. That trip, we began claiming and building loving systems everywhere around us.

I watched you embrace the work you loved, and by doing so, I watched you elevate community as we elevated you. It was only a matter of time for all these broken systems of oppression to collapse under their own weight, as we withdrew our consent and dependency and made them irrelevant in our culture, in our communities, and in the way we used love to govern our lives.

As bombs fell around us, we envisioned better, and more importantly, we did better. We fell in love countless times. We laughed, we cried, we knew we were worthy of utopia, as fire raged around us.

At the time, I was reminded of my own journey into love, and how bell hooks' *All About Love* gave me language and tools that were instrumental to bridging the gap between my engineering training and my experiences in social justice movements. It was also my introduction to using root cause analysis work on a personal, community, and structural level, all three areas deeply tied to one another.

An individual can take charge of their own life, despite the difficulty, without support. A community requires multiple community members to come together to create a transformative process and continue to invest in it.

Do you remember when it shifted? When it went from the community level to structural? Do you remember the teta uprisings? When they started the thousand-hour curfews, only allowing those above the age of seventy out at any time and the elders took to the streets and kickstarted the revolution?

They tried to break our connections with each other, but from the deep abyss they tried to plunge us into, we found immense love and gratitude for one another. It was the wake-up call so many needed, realizing the tools for transformation do not necessarily change. Even those elders who had not been 'political' could no longer ignore the state of the world.

Through love we create the conditions we deserve, recognizing that our people have for generations endured and survived by defiantly building these conditions of love.

We witnessed individuals using love to build community care, self-defense, and resilience, one at a time, each one a utopia attached to a constellation of others.

I still see their faces, all the elders martyred during the uprisings.

During those years of courage and loss, I learned that belonging is necessary to build hope. Spirituality is essential to build a loving community. Love is essential for belonging. Hope is essential to build spirituality. I realized then that when love, belonging, hope, and spirituality are braided together, no systems of oppression can survive them.

I laugh now at the bittersweet memory of that rebellion, the image of a Palestinian grandmother, strong and caring, with her do-not-fuck-with-me spirit. I also laugh because I've always been Teta.

Remember the hug? I asked if you wanted a hug and you said, "Yes," and I said, "Okay, but a real hug, like, for seven minutes." Within a few minutes, your breathing slowed down, your heart beating against mine. I will always cherish that.

Dear Reem 55

Thank you for loving me always, loving yourself, and moving toward nonattached love with me. Thank you for allowing me to remember, to write you a letter that has no actual beginning or end, no asks and no updates—just love.

With gratitude and spirit,
Yaffa

LETTER SIX
8/Cancer/26

Dear Home,

I write to you as I leave yet again, sorrow filling my heart as I remove myself from your walls, leaving behind memories and art that will be home to someone new. I still remember every time I have left—hundreds of times—yet this is the first time in over a dozen years. This has been my home, longer than any other home, nestled on a small hill north of Yaffa, where my grandfather had been born and would have died.

I have learned over the years to be home, regardless of the walls surrounding me, whether concrete, wood, car doors, the slightest of tent fabric, or even the outdoors under stars that I can or cannot see.

58   *Letters from a Living Utopia*

The world I grew up in had an abusive relationship with home, one of ownership and contempt and often filled with violence. We owned houses. We owned land. Everything was owned at one point or another. It was miserable to own a house and land as if they are yours and not their own entities with a life beyond humans.

How ridiculous it is to believe that we are or have ever been the center of the universe.

You have never been mine, I have always been a guest, the home within me able to honor the home within you. You are not four walls; you are not the land underneath your foundations. You are spirit gifting and hosting and for that I am eternally grateful.

Utopia is home, and home has never been dependent on the world outside of it. We are liberated when we are home.

The contradiction of language is what makes concepts powerful, for home is simultaneously a place and beyond a place.

I say goodbye to each tree individually, meditate to embrace the roots and communication systems that have existed for longer than humans have.

We first learn to belong while in the womb. The moment we take our first breath, we learn to assimilate—the antithesis to belonging.

***

My sisters were informed that I am not like them as soon as I was born. The difference was not that I was born in a different country or that Baba was nowhere to be found when I came into this world. It was not even that my name had

Dear Home 59

changed the moment I first cried. At less than two and four years of age, my older sisters had already learned that genitalia mattered more than gender. They understood what I did not, and although I understood things like death and oppression, I could not comprehend the concept of genitalia dictating gender. I don't think they could either, like most children, but what they did know was that we were different. Clearly, there was something wrong with me. They avoided me, and I learned to avoid myself.

I was born displaced, and in those first few years of life society demanded that I become displaced from body, mind, and spirit. As I grew older, I understood that in that world I had to be chipped at, piece by piece, until I was fully sculpted in their image.

This process was all too common, raging on daily in a world that was too afraid of those who were not chipped down to their prescribed and acceptable gender.

I learned about belonging through my relationship with the Divine, for even though so many who claim to pray to divinity tried to condition me to blame The Most Compassionate, I have always known otherwise. It was The Most Merciful who removed me from the clutches of rape and into a space where I would be in community. The Most Benevolent who swept me away again from a people that claimed to offer belonging when it was really their hunger for power and proximity to it that motivated them. The Most Gracious moved me across oceans so that I may be unmade. It was The Most Loving who allowed me to see that my shattered pieces were a part of a stained-glass masterpiece depicting the entire universe of being. I have always belonged in the embrace of

60   *Letters from a Living Utopia*

Divinity, knowing that I am divine and no one can ever take my belonging away from me.

As I began building spaces, I wondered why most around me had never experienced that level of divine belonging within themselves and through the greater universe and beyond.

At first, I thought I could provide that space for others, and I came close, before realizing this is not something anyone can grant for another. I can support others, I can build and constantly elevate, but I do not have the authority or power to grant belonging.

I have gone back and forth for over four decades, well into my sixties now in my learning and unlearning, claiming and unclaiming, remembering and forgetting and remembering again journeys in how the reality of belonging fits within my soul and in the fabric of universal truth. An emotion, a feeling, a space, a relationship, a way of life.

The English language is limited when it comes to understanding the fabrics of life. Is belonging limited to attachment, belonging *to*? In Arabic, the word for belonging is "انتماء." The root of this word is "نمي" which means "to grow," and even more so it means to "proliferate." It means "to thrive endlessly." A plant will still grow when suffocated in the dark and without much water. We grow despite being suffocated. We grow in conditions that deprive us. But when we belong, we grow with ease and peace.

When I say utopia is belonging, I am also saying utopia is proliferation, it is always thriving. Belonging is not an absence of difficulty or harm. Belonging is an endless supply of space to be all that we are meant to be in ways that rejuvenate instead of exhaust our spirits and soul.

Dear Home 61

Belonging does not have to be within community in the interpersonal sense. I learned most of what I know through witnessing, through learning from Black and Indigenous women's literature, through meditation and prayer and connection beyond life as represented in front of me in the various countries I have lived in.

Back then, I was never part of a community that I did not actively build. Now, every space is my community, regardless of where in the world I am and if anyone looks like me.

But back then things were different. For a time I desperately tried creating spaces to feel a sense of belonging, not realizing it was there all along. I learned to belong regardless of the external circumstances or acceptance around me. I learned to belong around sisters who hated my being. I belonged in spaces where I was not welcome. I belonged under the weight of transphobia, white supremacy, and classism for decades before the world order was broken and liberated.

I learned to belong under the rays of the sun making their way home into the depths of my skin. I belong everywhere. Thriving is a practice. Like hope and love, it requires rerouting our neuropathways to move past our conditioning away from it. I thrive.

It had taken me thirteen years, over four years of houselessness, living in nine countries, countless houses, two actual homes, loss of my entire family again and again, twenty-eight years worth of full-time employment in less than ten years (simultaneously holding three full-time jobs), navigating multiple immigration systems, hospitalized in three hospitals, being canceled, being disposed of repeatedly by family and friends and strangers, countless death threats, a few career

62   *Letters from a Living Utopia*

pivots, a handful of times nearly dying by suicide, police greeting me with guns in hand, pointed at me . . . to really grasp the concept of home.

Learning to claim home was what allowed my work to truly support me in claiming a liberated world.

Years before the revolution, I was only doing the work I yearned for. Even in the midst of multiple genocides, I always found home in my work. I was nonattached to the work I did. I got to show up, do things, and let go. I may have lived month-to-month and never had savings, but I was doing well, my survival was stable.

It wasn't that the barriers and systems of oppression did not exist for me, they did. It was the recognition that I will always be more than they are. They can kill me, they can extract my labor, they can harm my loved ones, but beyond that what do they have? What do they have when I have the ability to connect to trees, the sea, the land underneath my feet, land across oceans, stars above, and so much more? They may burn trees, but even they have never been able to colonize the stars. I have never been a single person, and when you're a community made of humans, land, stars, and spirit, there's no ending you.

I had built a life where survival did not take up the majority of my mental real estate. I thrived within myself endlessly. I belonged within myself and in this universe. And I was and still am nonattached to a body, mind, or any other specific form of existence. I belong beyond the barriers to belonging.

I learned that belonging is utopic, and is not rooted in imperialist, capitalist, patriarchal society.

Dear Home 63

You are the home of a different time though. I met you as the dust was settling after the revolution, as we were still clearing bodies and figuring out next steps. You have been my partner throughout. You were my first home.

For years, I had struggled to belong anywhere when I could not be home. The same home that Darwish asks in a poem, "What in life is worth living for?" and the answer is always Falasteen. As a displaced individual, I have struggled with being accepted for everything that I am when the land beneath my feet is mourning the loss of Indigenous sovereignty. I have struggled with my role at the intersections of displacement and settlerism.

Over time, I began defining belonging as being accepted for everything that I am or can ever be.

To cultivate belonging is to begin laying the foundation for how we are in utopia. There is no marginalization in utopia, there is no queerness in the sense that anyone is punished for who they are. No one is invisible. Everyone is home in every sense of the word.

If I could go back in time and tell folks before liberation one thing, it would be to find belonging. There is no utopia without it. Before liberation, I would ask folks if they were ready to live in a liberated world, if they knew how to. I was met with silence again and again, we were not yet ready. Belonging is what made us ready.

I was ready for you because of the decades of work I did to be ready. Thank you for embracing and welcoming me.

Yaffa

LETTER SEVEN
27/Pisces/16

Dear Rest,

Do you remember everyday life during capitalism? The uncertainty, humiliation, the feeling of powerlessness, the heaviness underneath eyelids, the friction of bones misaligned, the scent of flesh nearly burning from fluorescent lights in cubicles where our spirits died?

Capitalism made us merchants of injustice, trading in death we didn't know our own value depended on. Most of all it was the feeling of sinking in quicksand, every movement digging you deeper, slipping in place for a lifetime.

It may seem like a strange starting point, yet I know from the flutter of my heart that you will also recognize why we must start here.

I think about you often, the extension of space that allows rest to exist within my soul. I didn't think about you growing up when I was displaced and plunged into a world of alienation. All I knew was Mama needed to get another job so I could get a root canal.

Around me, people claimed rest was absence, if you went away on vacation (a foreign concept to us barely surviving on food stamps), or if you had "lazy" days. I didn't know any rest. My hours and days away from school were filled with grocery shopping or emptiness. The emptiness expanded in high school, an hour of school and then emptiness locked within four walls, insomnia and fainting, unbreakable cycles that left me sedated most of the time. Houseless at seventeen, the cycle continued, hyper-alert on one end but banking one memory for every few months as if I was being transported through time and space, between countries, between couches, between park benches, between people, between death, always between but never long enough to remember. Then three jobs, then four, then five, then graduation, and three full-time jobs, then two full-time jobs, then . . . There was no rest.

Days off from work were just days for other jobs. It was during those days I thought rest was Korean spas, massages, any momentary escape no matter how small to allow my body to continue operating. Between three hundred flights a year, I found myself tied to a cane to get by. Always barely getting by.

One day, after eighteen hours organizing mutual aid at the start of the COVID-19 pandemic in 2020, I couldn't do it anymore. My body had broken years prior, my mind had

Dear Rest 67

snapped beyond comprehension, but my spirit broke then too. It wasn't just the community conflict that catalyzed it. It was being told that despite all that work, I still hadn't shown up for community—by people who had done almost nothing.

I left, to yet another country, to colonized Northern Ireland (Éire) this time. I had a full scholarship and worked as a consultant to pay for any additional expenses those two years. Finally, rest had arrived in the form of free time. I read when I wanted. I walked when I wanted. Within months, I retired the cane that offered companionship for the majority of the previous three years. My body slowly began healing.

I left Éire to be the caretaker for a sister with stage-four cancer. Six months later I flew to Indonesia and thought I would never fly again. My body had been healing for over two years, but my mind had not, snapping too far. I could no longer tell time and space apart. Seeing something that triggered a memory from years prior I would find myself in a portal, my current reality suddenly crashing into the past. In an instant, friends I met in 2022 were with me traveling in 2018. Dead friends were alive again.

I don't think I would have made it back if not for the hundreds of hours of intensive yoga for over a month and a half. Yoga reconnected parts of my mind and body with spirit in a way that had not happened in decades. I got back and I rested my body and my mind again, this time not as a caretaker, not traveling endlessly. I did yoga everyday by the lake, my skin finally feeding from the sunlight so desperately lacking in Éire and N'dakinna.

Then October 7, 2023 happened. I take a deep breath writing this, taking in the others surrounding me, writing, drawing, singing, doing whatever it is that feeds their soul—in community. October 7th was one of many unequivocal reality shifts that we experienced back then.

As I write this, I am remembering waking up one morning in Aida Camp in Bethlehem ten months after that day. The Al-Tab'een massacre had occurred hours earlier; over one hundred people—each with their roles and dreams—were shredded into nothingness. This was 'normal' back then. That morning, I created a social media post talking about how as we show up, we build the community needed for liberation.

For ten months prior, I was learning something: rest is not what capitalism told us it was. At a time when many were moving toward and prioritizing rest as a radical form of protest, I felt that the definition being centered was a capitalistic one.

Within capitalism, we were taught that work and life are two separate entities. We are meant to suffer within work. Patriarchy, white supremacy, imperialism have told us we must suffer during our lives. It was capitalism that told us work is meant to be misery.

It sounds counterintuitive. Why would capitalism want us to hate work? Capitalism only existed through our labor after all.

But if you could believe that work can be restful and joyful, you might not wish to participate within a system that uses and abuses you any longer. Similarly, an abusive partner will make sure you believe everyone else is a monster. Believing in better is the most powerful thing.

Within this definition, rest is a complete separation from work. This fails to capture two transformative aspects of work: first, work is our contribution to our community. Secondly, work is not what pays us to survive in capitalism.

Dear Rest 69

***

I had learned years prior, through working multiple full-time jobs simultaneously, that we can get paid for what we would do naturally within our communities and that can serve as a means of survival. It does not have to be either/or. This took me the equivalent of twenty years of full-time work to be able to achieve, but it's possible.

For many of us at the margins, our being was our work. At the time, my work with queer and trans Muslims and Palestinians could never be separated from who I am as a queer and trans Muslim Palestinian. Separating me from my work was the same as separating me from my purpose of living.

Instead, I utilized a concept of rest built from my understanding of Islam, Palestinian culture, and Chinese medicine through yin yoga.

Rest is stillness within. We are taught to run from the things that we are uncomfortable with. My culture teaches me to sit with the things that make me uncomfortable. Yin yoga is a practice of stillness that allows us to engage the deepest parts of our muscle tissue in a way that other yoga practices do not. It is in stillness that we go deep. It is in stillness that the transformation occurs. It is not in separation or in immediate action that only addresses the surface level.

In Islam, I was taught to pray when I have a challenge. Prayer, however, is not a way to solve anything, nor is it a way to run away. It is a spiritual and physical practice to sit within.

This is not to say that distance is never necessary; it absolutely can be, but it does not have to be the only option. Sitting in discomfort, in grief, in pain, in whatever is tearing us apart, allows us to dig deeper to a level where we can transform what we're sitting with. Constantly moving to and from rarely leads to transformation, and we find ourselves in the same position again and again.

Separating us from our community, from the things that move us forward, is not restful.

Many came to similar conclusions following October 7th as they had during other crises. To move us away from community is to not allow us to rest. It was during this time that I realized that rest is not all-encompassing and holistic, there are different kinds of rest and these require different interventions. Resting our body is not the same as resting our minds and not the same as resting our souls. I can rest my body through sleep, through bodywork, through healthy food, etc. However, a massage will not heal genocide. After the ninety-minute massage, my body is able to carry more, but I am not rested.

Resting my mind at the time could look like doing work that fed my soul and inspired me, it looked like breaks between meetings, breaks in general, but that does not rest the unease in my soul. Resting my soul, for me, can only happen in community.

I reflect on my community around me right now, creatives and artists who inspire me. I look further to the olive trees and orange trees dotting the sides, land that knows my blood like it knows itself.

The first time I was able to enter Falasteen my soul began healing and I found myself soaring in ways I did not know were possible without community. I was home. Home heals.

That same trip I reflected on seeing fruit sold on the side of the road, Baba's voice in my ears saying never to buy fruit that had been sitting in the sun for too long. I reflected on

Dear Rest 71

how the sun is what gives life to fruit while it is on a tree—it cannot grow without it. But that same sun, when the fruit is far from itself and its community, will speed up the aging process for the fruit, rotting it quicker.

Being in community allows us to rest during the worst of times.

For years after, I witnessed how almost no one in our community was doing well, except those who found purpose and direction.

I remember the shift in my life when I pivoted my work to support the worldbuilders, as I like to call them. It was an organic transition without a beginning or an end, something I had always done but had not named until the years that followed the riots a couple of years after October 7th.

As someone with Cancer in their twelfth house, I can dream easily, separating my mind from my body and existing somewhere else as reprieve. Rest was truly a space deep within me, not external. I didn't realize that wasn't the case for everyone. It was during one of those journeys, as I walked along my newly created forest of rage, a whale I had been in a previous life swimming in the ocean above me, I mourned the extension of rest that holds us in our consciousness and subconscious, between awareness and sleep, and between every moment of life. In that world, rest is not separate from life. Life is restful. What a drastic difference from where I was years prior where the only rest was going to be when I was dead. "But what if life was restful?" I asked as I danced among the stars.

What if life was restful? What if we all had home? What is that world like and who is building that world? I could picture them, across generations, individuals and communities who dedicated their being to this world, and I wondered who took care of us, knowing full well that very few even try. So I decided to try. I couldn't take anyone into my inner worlds, but I could help the worldbuilders in my life survive capitalism and have housing, medical care, psychosocial and somatic support, spiritual care, skill-building, archiving, and anything else they needed.

Not a lot changed. I just claimed a possibility.

The possibility was you, rest, and I dedicated my life to you, to living you. In a world where we rest in deep connection, we find liberation together.

Now we know this, you are life. We know rest is sitting with an olive tree with friends and partners or alone or with strangers. Rest is sitting underneath the stars knowing they're recharging us. Rest is home.

In gratitude, may we always find you,
Yaffa

LETTER EIGHT
28/Leo/32

Dear Little One,

I sit here in gratitude for you, lighting incense and sage, drinking mint-and-sage tea, and wearing my most intricate thobe for our conversation today. I cleaned the house today, for your arrival, my knees aching in a way they haven't in over a decade. It took hours, a nap in between, remembering memories through touch and smell. There were some mild protests from loved ones, but they knew what today meant for me.

It is our ninety-ninth birthday, something neither of us ever thought we would reach, not expecting to live past our thirty-second.

74 *Letters from a Living Utopia*

I want to start by thanking you for accepting my invitation to join me in my home after all this time, on the day our solar and lunar years align. I will visit you at your home until the very end, where we will be united with spirit for the final time, the final utopia. I have lived a lifetime of utopias, in worlds where others would say utopia is the furthest thing from reality and in worlds where utopias were lived for everyone.

I used to believe that you would either replace me or disappear entirely as we built our relationship and healed. I laugh now at my silliness and my lack of knowledge of relationship-building at the time.

I saw you first through a mirror, although I had been talking to you for months prior. You looked like the twenty year old that I was, but I knew you were still a child of four. I talked to you for years before you talked back, and I'm grateful for the silence you gifted our relationship, as I learned to name the relationship I yearned for. It was more than a year later, as I struggled with abandonment that I finally claimed that you are in fact real. I've always known you were real, but to find you named in abandonment trauma healing books and even artistic reclamation work meant you weren't another reflection due to psychosis—real either way but in a way that others could understand. But there you were, named in books and practices, and then you spoke to me.

I had started taking some time to connect with you, just the two of us. I would take you to the movies, playgrounds, hikes, swimming, coloring, journaling, or whatever else I thought you might enjoy. I tried to be gentle and kind, never pressuring you to talk back.

Dear Little One 75

Then I remember meditating, picturing you lost and needing to be found. I found you, between buildings torn from the ground, more rubble than sky, in the corner sheltering. You didn't look scared. You didn't look tired. You looked resolute, apathetic, untouchable. I wanted to embrace you, protect you, but you looked like you could—and *would*—protect me. My heart broke, from my chest to yours. Maybe you spoke to take care of me, maybe you were finally ready to accept care. Either way, we learned to care for one another.

We continued our time together and then started talking at different times of the day. You shared insights I didn't have.

Years of work and several intensive treatments later, I saw you during a meditation in a glass prison. I knew you were about to break free, and I thought you would be free to move a bit more. Instead, as the glass shattered, an entire universe formed, wheatgrass fields and constellations. You moved into the safest part of me and expanded it in ways that I couldn't even imagine. You moved home then, and I continued moving toward home.

Now, I am home and I am remembering that utopia is similar to the glass cage you were held in and the world beyond that you have lived in since. I think about this now as I wait for you, thinking about all that we have been through, every transition, all the lifetimes, and here we are toward the end or the beginning. And although I am not attached to what comes next, a part of me wonders if it's similar to the glass box you were in, the one I experienced moving into liberation.

I close my eyes, inhale deeply, and feel you coming into my space.

> Yaffa: "Hi, my love."
>
> Little One: "I can come back later if you're busy."
>
> Yaffa: "I have been waiting for this for ninety-nine years. I've waited enough."

We both laugh.

> Little One: "Okay, I guess I'll stay. Thanks for inviting me."
>
> Yaffa: "Nawarat, literally the sun came out through the clouds for you."

I say this, feeling the sun's rays on my skin for the first time today. You roll your eyes and I laugh.

> Little One: "What did you want to talk about?"
>
> Yaffa: "I want to talk about what comes next."
>
> Little One: "You come home."

I smile and they look away.

> Yaffa: "But what does that mean?"
>
> Little One: "It means no more visits. You come home, we return home."
>
> Yaffa: "I can ask more, but I know we'll go around in circles, language seems so inadequate."
>
> Little One: "Language isn't real. I'm not telling you words, I am telling you things only your soul understands and has to simplify for you. It's not real, it's not enough."
>
> Yaffa: "Yeah, I know, you're right. Isn't it silly to try?"

Dear Little One

> Little One: "It's not. You yearn for something you have known yet in your current form cannot name or truly understand and you know you will go there again."

It's not the first time. You were scared of utopia too.

> Yaffa: "Yeah, even as I talked about it. It was scary. How would I run away in utopia? What would I do if I don't need to fix it?"

I learned though.

> Little One: "Every soul does."
>
> Yaffa: "Can you give me any advice to live the rest of the time?"
>
> Little One: "Time is silly. You will die soon, but soon isn't real. Humans are wasteful, expecting things. That's why I like you, you've learned nonattachment. Anything else is silly. You will come home and you're already home with me. You have already died and you're alive. You are all at once and spread out. You are not you until you are you."
>
> Yaffa: "I know, I know, I'm tired and there's only so much more that I can say but I have a final question. What made us have faith in utopia?"
>
> Little One: "We were always meant to. Faith isn't something you have or do, it just is. Faith is accepting what you do not know instead of only focusing on what you know. We didn't know him, but he was there. We did know him and there was still pain. We missed him and he could've been anywhere. Faith is letting go, it's nonattachment. I know you constantly talk about it, but it's actually simple. Let go of what should and shouldn't be. That's what we've always done."

Yaffa: "We have always done that, haven't we?"

Little One: "Well I have, I remember a lot of times you did not, including recently, but that's also not the point. Just because you didn't practice nonattachment that one time doesn't mean you have no faith. It's like being a river, and sometimes you need to resist the pull to move in a different direction. Faith is knowing the river will get you there, but there are countless theres. You don't control any of them, but sometimes you may want to rest. I know, I'm brilliant, now please go get some food and nap. I have a date with Qaher and she does not like to be kept waiting. Thank you for the visit. I'll see you at home."

We hug, they leave, and I fall asleep with ease. I smile for a long time when my body begins to rise again, their being just a moment away. I think about going to visit them and then I think better of it, instead deciding to transcribe the rest of this letter.

There's nothing that I can teach you, Little One, as one of my chosen sisters used to call me, the only one who treated me like a younger sibling before we lost contact over seventy years ago. And you are right, as you always are. It's funny, people think I'm wise, but they've never met you. If I am wise, it is only because I am in relationship with you.

I'm grateful for our journey, grateful that you named faith and nonattachment.

I had thought a lot about utopia my entire life and although I knew that I would never truly be able to envision it because I had not lived it yet, I'd had some thoughts. So, when I was able to move home and be a part of the rebuilding process in Falasteen, it was as if I had been in a glass box and

Dear Little One 79

that box exploded into a million pieces, opening the door to an entire universe beyond anything I could imagine. This feels like a similar moment. I am grateful for your companionship on this journey and the faith we carry for whatever comes next.

I remember being shocked that you always had the answer to all my questions. You were my first real best friend, the one who stayed alive with me as everyone else around me died or was killed.

I learned to have faith alongside you.

I grew up in a community that had faith—in Allah, in one another, and in the land surrounding us.

Islam and my Indigenous practices have taught me it is faith that builds utopia, not trust (at least not in the way we use it). Even now, years into liberated Falasteen and the world it liberated with it, trust creeps into spaces in the ways it was previously weaponized. Do you remember when trust was weaponized in interpersonal relationships and community-building practices and so many other places? Remember all those years balking at the idea of 'building at the speed of trust'?

At times, trust was seen as a precursor to relationship-building. I understand why that was the case, especially when the lack of safety was very real. Trust requires us to prove ourselves. In a systemically oppressive society, that was often equated with justifying our humanity.

Instead of using trust as a pathway for collaboration and community-building, it was often used as a way to gate keep and create barriers to system transformation.

Faith, on the other hand, allows us to honor the things we cannot name, the memories that are no longer ours, and

80   *Letters from a Living Utopia*

an understanding that although we are visionaries, we are not in control of outcomes.

In Latin, the words "faith," "trust," and "belief" are all intrinsically tied. In Arabic, both trust and faith have multiple words to represent the different dimensions of each.

In Arabic, the main word for faith is "إيمان." Faith in Arabic is rooted in safety. It is not trust that creates safety, it is faith. Since we do not have power over safety, trust is *not* attainable.

Faith is nonattachment to outcomes. Faith is living without answers or knowledge of what you're meant to expect because none of us know what to expect on the best of days.

Faith allows us to be fully open to receive all that another entity is meant to transmit to us through the universe. It is not about the other person because we are nonattached to an outcome with a single individual. If this person harms us, then we move on.

Operating outside of faith is operating from a place of fear of harm from everyone. Harm is out there. We will never know fully how we will interact with anyone and pretending like we can control that means we are never receiving all we can be. I say these things to honor the journey we have been on. Remember my fear of everyone?

I think there was even a time I was afraid of you, the knowledge you held, and wondering if I was ready to truly understand my being and the world around me. I didn't know if I was ready, but I jumped in with you on our healing journey anyway. As we were rebuilding the world, so many thought it was impossible to truly move into collective liberation. We believed—we had faith.

Dear Little One 81

I would not be connected to you if not for faith. There were many back then who believed talking to your inner child was "not real." This was the same world that believed hearing and seeing things others do not was bad. It is faith that allows us to connect beyond ourselves and access spirituality.

I think that's why I pushed back against trust back then. Trust seemed ableist and elitist.

***

The final revolution was built on faith. We came together, recognizing that each of us was capable of a different kind of faith, belief, and trust than what we were conditioned by systems of oppression. It was in a world where we all had access to our inner children, to the land around us, to every aspect of the human in all of us and how that was reflected across the Milky Way looking down on us, as we sat in the dark after the power went out.

It was when we started believing that liberation is not just possible but probable that we stopped resisting the freefall toward liberation. It was not until we moved beyond intentions, beyond our old ways of moving through conflict, as we claimed love and belonging, as we claimed liberation instead of waiting for the ruling classes to grant it.

The Arabic word for intention is "نِيّة," which has the same root as "date pit, fruit kernel, and core" and also "remoteness and distance." In English, its etymology comes from the Italian word *intendere*, which means "to turn one's attention"; or in the physical sense, "to stretch out."

In our current use of intentionality, it is the process of bringing consciousness in. In a way, it still holds true to the

English root. We are stretching out our subconscious into our consciousness. What's missing for me is found in the Arabic translation.

Why do we need to stretch out our subconscious in the first place? What was preventing it from already being stretched out? How are we maintaining balance as we stretch out? Are we perhaps covering other areas in the process?

There are so many questions that arise in this beautiful process. If we know what leads us to setting our intentions, if we go into the "pit," or the root of intentions, we are able to ensure that our efforts are aligned, true, and transformative.

Back then, we threw words around as if they meant nothing and everything all at the same time. I was guilty of this, constantly talking about community but never knowing who community referred to.

I was an engineer once upon a time. In my engineering school, root cause analyses were instrumental to every part of our training. We were told scientists understand problems and engineers solve them. For years after, I wondered why the two were not married together more often, for it is not enough to go to the root. Reflecting on our root chakra and how it corresponds with our third eye is a great example of this. Focusing entirely on the root prevents us from seeing the big picture. We must balance both, recognize the kernel and see the entire fruit, the tree that bore it, and everything that allowed it to exist.

You helped me balance both, reminding me years ago: "Who told you that you have to build utopia alone?"

I learned to find the things that excited me, things community needed. I found others who complemented them, others who brought things that I never knew possible, and

Dear Little One 83

others who brought similar things because why carry an entire branch on your own?

Decades ago, I used to write feverishly, often publishing four to eight books a year when few trans Palestinians were given platforms to speak. Over the years, that amount went down, lower and lower, until I stopped publishing altogether. I still have a lot to say, but publishing was never about my voice being centered—it was about making sure our voices were honored. Now they are, so many voices, so many archives and stories shared. My dream of being a single voice among millions is now a reality. I smile as my voice fades into the background as so many others swell.

Thank you for carrying the branch with me! It was through you that I learned that community can be found within and with faith, even when it is not abundant on the outside. Today, I am in balance, internally and externally in community, but it is you I want to share space with. You are my first and last community. Someday death will come to carry us both home, and I am honored that it'll be you there in the very end.

With all my love, root and all, to you, from,
Me

LETTER NINE
19/Aquarius/1

Dear Malak,

Do you remember our conversation in your kitchen my first night in Haifa? We had quite a few conversations that night, and the years have clouded them all. But this one remains singular in my mind. Specifically, the conversation about being *of* community. Many people at the time would say they defined themselves within community, but you were the first one who truly did.

I think about you today after class. These last few months, since coming back home, I find myself working with children aged five to seven. We relaunched the new unschooling model, and although I was initially training

86 *Letters from a Living Utopia*

parents, I wanted some time with the kids themselves to be able to monitor growth on both ends. We're learning that parents and children have to be taught synchronously. I've done this before, years ago, but now we're also breaking apart the old definitions of parenting and moving toward community caretaking structures. It's been a lot, but you can probably guess that I'm smiling as I write this, loving every challenge.

Anyway, these last several months we've been spending more and more time in the olive and orange groves, as well as growing new saplings for the years to come. We've grown figs, apricots, pomegranates, loquats, blood oranges, sage, poppies, and so many other things in the gardens that now fill the space where the downtown used to be. New sidewalks opened up that trace where the roads used to be, filled now with jasmine bushels surrounding trees, herbs growing all around them. We had the parents work on breaking down the roads and moving the trees, then the community came together to plant the rest. Now, everyone takes care of them, the gardens between the cafes and restaurants that have been here for hundreds of years. It looks nothing like it used to, but it looks like home. I am excited for your visit soon, and I cannot wait for the time I can travel north to Haifa to see you and what you've done to restore Arus El-Bahar ("The Bride of The Sea") to its endless glory.

My main focus, with both the adult caretakers and the children, is establishing a foundation for collectivism and self-actualization. It's amazing to see how easy it's been to develop this foundation working with the land and moving away from the systems of oppression we were raised with. I wish we had this as children, but even without it, we still

Dear Malak 87

managed to find our way to these things in our lifetime, and I am grateful.

I'm remembering our conversation as I share my knowledge with the community, many of whom had also learned to claim collectivism and self-actualization in the years leading up to the revolution, but I was surprised to find that as the systems of oppression fell, it felt like folks were tempted to step back into individualism. Thankfully, many of us noticed and some of us knew to expect this and we've been able to work together to address it.

Back when we first met, over two decades ago, I was mostly surrounded by global majority queer and trans organizers, all of whom *claimed* to be collectivist and not individualistic but did not yet know how to dismantle the culture of individualism that embodied so many aspects of their language, relationality, sense of self, and obligations to others. But I noticed early on in our relationship that every decision you made was about the community, not yourself, even though you didn't use the word "collectivism."

That first evening we talked about how we would not enter any kind of intimate relationship unless it served the community, that our standard for who we partner with was rooted in our expectation that people be able to take care of themselves and others and impact community positively. We talked about how wellness is stigmatized and how redefining self-actualization is critical to how we move in the world. We talked about healing as a responsibility to community, not only ourselves.

That single conversation has been the blueprint for a lot of the work we've been doing the last several months. I wanted to share some of those thoughts with you because I know you get just as excited about this work as I do, and to say I love and miss you.

Years ago, I had looked for the basic definition of the word "healing" and found it meant "to be whole." In Arabic, the word for healing, "شفاء," means to "recuperate." At the time, I wondered what we were recuperating. Have we ever been whole before? Are we returning to that wholeness through our healing processes? These are the questions I ask now and had asked for decades ago in training.

The word for self-actualization is "الذات." There is no exact translation for it, but in a sense, it is enlightenment. It is the highest level beyond consciousness and subconsciousness, where we are one with the universe. In the yogic and tantric traditions of Hinduism, it would translate to Kundalini or Samadhe. In Buddhist practice, it is Samyaksaṃbodhi.

We are only able to achieve this when we are whole.

Self-actualization is healing. Healing is wholeness. Self-actualization is wholeness.

Earlier today, we saw something that inspired me to write this letter. We were taking a break for lunch, sitting in the shade and eating the mujadara that some of the community members made for us when Razan gasped and pointed toward a butterfly that was fluttering about erratically on the ground a few feet away. I was so proud of the kids in that moment, for no one rushed into action, allowing us to witness and not disrupt nature. There were two other butterflies hovering above and they kept swooping down toward the butterfly on the ground. I wondered if maybe one of us had stepped on this butterfly, damaging its wings, or if something else had happened.

Dear Malak 89

To the surprise of everyone, including myself, the two other butterflies lifted the crawling butterfly and the three flew together slowly, moving around in a circle. They started flying fast and faster, until suddenly the butterfly being carried started flying on its own. The three flew away together, and we all sat there in silence for a bit. And, of course, I brought this up in the class after lunch, but I don't think I really needed to. They know that healing and self-actualization are about the community, not an individual. We care for one another, we rise together. We did rise together. They know wholeness is not about or for a single person, it is essential for everyone.

Working with the adults has been a little trickier.

As you know, the last decade or so has been about moving beyond our egos, into collectivism and shared responsibility for collective liberation. We did that—or at least enough people did that for the revolution to be successful, but not everyone did and even the ones who did, were (are?) scared. Our world ended, so it makes sense that so many would try to move toward what they're comfortable with, but what we were comfortable with was authority concentrated in violent institutions. Of course, the worldbuilders and culture workers knew this, and we knew to address it immediately, but that doesn't mean it's been easy. I smile again, as I know you know how exciting this has been for me.

We have been discussing the concept of self-actualization without the ego.

What is self-actualization when the self is not about an individual? Of course, before we got to this question, we had to break down the definition of individual within a collectivist context. We had to break down that caring for your family and close friends is still individualistic, not collectivist. They knew this, I know this, and we both know pushback happened anyway. I am so grateful for it. When I was met with resistance, I knew that we were actually getting to the root we needed to truly do this work.

Once we got to a place where we were able to recognize that community isn't about who we are in relationships with but rather everyone and everything, most importantly things we will never know, we were able to go into defining the self. Within so many of our upbringings, the self was a singular concept. It was the "I." We had to break it down to recognize that the self is a part of everything; be it divinity, the universe, or even the on-the-ground ecosystem surrounding us. "I" is not about a person—after all, we are made of recycled bodies that come from the land and are born carrying ancestors and spirit within us. Our thoughts are gifted to us and passed down over countless generations. Stars sing to the stardust within us. Where is the "I"? It's the entire constellation that we are, and therefore it's so much more than we perceive as mere individuals.

That part is always fun to discuss, and now it makes so much more sense after witnessing its power during the revolution.

Self-actualization is not about separating the self from the whole and centering what is best for one. There is no such thing as best for one. Removing the ego returns the self to wholeness, where we actualize within the universe.

I didn't share this with you when we first met but years prior to our meeting, I wrote an article about how that adage of "placing your mask on first before helping others in the case of an emergency" is only rooted in Global North society.

Dear Malak

In many cultures, placing a mask on others is what gives the individual inspiration to place a mask on themselves when they are part of the whole. I love this conversation too, especially as we've been expanding who cares for whom and we break away from the parent/child dynamic.

What happens if all healing/self-actualization practice honors that the work is not about an individual but is about everything?

We shared examples of how this can look and has looked in the past, recognizing that all of us have always had a deep part of us that has been collectivist and yearning for true self-actualization.

I shared that I healed for my inner child and to be a healthy person for my sisters and loved ones. I healed further to claim a liberated Falasteen, decades before it was liberated.

My healing practice has always been about those around me and the wider community and world beyond that. I do not heal for myself. If I had tried, I am sure I would be dead right now. The closest I have gotten to healing for myself is healing the parts of me that have come before and will come after. I do not view myself as a linear being, unchanging. I learned that time is a circle and wholeness is a spiral along the way. When we think of wholeness, we think of a full circle and not an arrow shooting off into the distance. But wholeness is not linear.

I was asked how my healing practice has transformed since liberation. I tell them healing itself has never changed, what changed is how we move together. It is easy to remember that I am part of a whole today because I am actually part of a whole. But back then, I was part of an invisible whole lacking community but requiring faith.

Back then, healing was often thought of as healing *from*, as if every arena of healing must be linked to something named from our experiences. We left so little room for the things beyond us.

During a trip last week, we entered an orange grove north of Yaffa and I felt a sense of sadness witnessing the abandoned mansions along the coast. As I looked around, I noticed that suddenly everyone was quiet, barely moving as they stared at the trees around us. A tear streamed down my cheek and sat with grief amidst the grove. We all cried without knowing why. We didn't need to know why. It was only on the way back that I realized this grove was the same one my grandfather's family had stewarded one hundred years ago, before the Nakba. But we all felt it, the land grieving so much in those hundred years until we came back home. I honor the grove and the service of my ancestors—I witnessed it and let it be.

I learned long ago that I don't need to solve every mystery—the knowledge that's meant for me will find me, and what is not will not be. We talked about the unknown that night, do you remember?

Later that night we were shrouded in a conversation about Islam and spirituality. One of my favorite things about Islam is its embrace of the unknown. In Islam, humans are not the only conscious beings in the universe. We do not know who else might be out there beyond our recognition of Jinn. Even then, there is so much unknown about Jinns and we are never meant to know. There's joy in embracing the unknown, not as a mystery that needs to be solved but as a mystery that is not meant for us to solve.

Dear Malak 93

I wrote this poem years ago that I only recently found again, a sheet of paper tucked away among my different poetry collections. It was written during the Cancer new moon nearly two decades ago, which at the time was subsequently the Islamic New Year. I reflected on a year of reflection that was about savoring uncertainty.

Mysteries

I live in
shadow
breathe in
the light
bathing in
knowledge and
wisdom in
the unknown

I have never
been into
mysteries
but I am
enamored by
the mysteries
of the universe

Alive in the
unknown
never yearning
to understand it

Home between
the known and
unknown

I emphasize the humbleness of knowing and not knowing when we begin and end every class. We know what we know. We learn what we learn from one another. But the vast majority of things are not known to us, some never will be, others will come with living. We're already witnessing magic that we couldn't have predicted.

The greatest mysteries are those that we are not meant to solve or even try solving. We are not meant to figure everything out. There will always be things we don't remember, conflicts we don't resolve, universal knowledge we will not access. Nonattachment to figuring it all out allows us to live in balance.

For everything I know, I equally do not know. I have no urges to accumulate knowledge, comfortable in what I do know and faithful in the belief that knowledge finds me when it desires to. That knowledge becomes wisdom when it serves a greater purpose.

Wholeness is the same way. There is so much we do not know about this spiral, we move to wholeness not regardless of, but with an appreciation for, the spirit that guides us and rises beyond us.

I learned a lesson years ago that I have been bringing into my work since: that healing happens through belonging and love. In a space of belonging, when we feel like we will be accepted for everything we are or can ever be, and we feel held in community, we heal even if we do not narrate the specifics of our own experiences. Similarly, love as an investment in spiritual growth concludes cycles of pain without ever having to discuss or confront our pain because love is the response we would have wanted when the pain was first inflicted. When we receive what we need, we heal.

Dear Malak 95

Healing in community is being in spaces of belonging and love.

Thank you for the space of belonging and love all those years ago. I still remember our conversations and see your work with youth back then as the prism for all possibilities. Healing and self-actualization are always about the community; nothing can change that!

Thank you for being the first person to reflect these understandings back to me!

With gratitude,
Yaffa

LETTER TEN
13/Libra/17

To everyone who has harmed me,

I haven't thought of you in years. I feel a sense of gratitude and pride in the world I belong in today. I am grateful for my ability to have released so much that I'm now here, in between the olive trees that dot the coast as if yearning for the sea themselves.

I wonder how you are, if you have felt the same release, and I send you love across this sea and ocean, wherever you may be today. I look out to the sea, the cliffs of Yaffa behind me, Teta's family's old factory hovering above as if rising with the sun from the east. It's brisk, and I tighten my sheepskin around me and send gratitude to all life.

98 *Letters from a Living Utopia*

It took a long time before you were no longer on my mind. After all, the harm you caused left wounds that festered and refused to scar over. You existed across different timelines and geographic locations in my life, but your patterns were ones that I witnessed thousands of times both before and after liberation.

Over the years I have taken the wounds you caused, opened them, and weaved *tatreez* patterns over them that brought me home. I have learned a lot from these wounds and the healing process that followed, every stitch a life lesson that allowed me to find my way here today.

I recognized years ago that utopia is about forgiveness. That we are not liberated through attachment. The act of letting go is instrumental in weaving a liberated world. Today I see it in every interaction. I see people navigating accountability. I see forgiveness happening with or without accountability.

In the before times, I used to believe that forgiveness happened with the most basic versions of accountability, for myself of course, as my definition for community was more demanding when it came to harm caused to others. I desired an apology, an acknowledgment of action, and the barest minimum of plans to avoid the same behavior again.

It was too much to ask, of you and so many others.

I did not ask for you to take back the rape, the housing insecurity, the hospitalization, the near deportation, the disposal, and all the rest. I just wanted an acknowledgment. In a way, I wanted to be validated. I wanted to validate that I existed, that you existed, and that we existed momentarily across the same time and place.

To everyone who has harmed me   99

I mourned possibilities of relationships before I truly understood how to honor my grief, move through it, and claim nonattachment to release it. I have wished you well over the years, and for that I am grateful.

I learned through nonattachment that I cannot control any outcomes or anyone else's decisions. I cannot control whether or not another person walks toward accountability.

For years prior, I carried every wound, keeping them ripe and moist for when that accountability finally comes my way. Blame my Cancer moon or blame the fact that most people forget too quickly and someone has to be the record keeper, and all of that is me. Or was me.

As I write this, I watch the waves of the sea crashing into the rocks underneath and then retreating in an endless cycle of releasing and clearing. I learned to release and clear along the way.

I am grateful that my work has always centered community and through that work I can hold myself accountable to the same standards I sought to invest into our communities. An apology was enough for me, but for a community I desired transformation. Before liberation we called this "transformative justice," now we just call it "life." I know you know this, and I hope that you learned to witness your hypocrisy in using language that you never practiced then. I hope you are practicing it now or at the very least learning to with your communities as I am in mine.

I reflect on years in a world bombarded by violence and harm, celebrations of genocide, and constant layers of oppression—a capitalist, white supremacist utopia. You were birthed in that world; your harm was cultivated in that utopia.

100   *Letters from a Living Utopia*

I think about you today because of an interaction I had yesterday. Ayman came into one of the grief and revitalization spaces I facilitate and for two hours cried as we held her. This morning, we walked along the water, dipping our toes in and out of the sea, grounding and transcending as we spoke about experiences from the capitalist, white supremacist utopia we left behind so long ago. We spoke about healing. Like the waves, it flows, pushing in and pulling out, and even when it seems as if we are done, it recedes to uncover deeper layers that we may not be aware of. Ayman woke up two days ago with a new layer that demanded attention.

We talked about carrying the weight of hundreds of years of violence in our bodies, minds, and spirits. That even back then we wept with the mountains, rivers, oceans, and everything in between at least a few times a year. She shared the weight of a society that has told us we do not exist and has tried to destroy everything we are every day of our lives. A utopia where families are a part of that violence and must pretend as if folks should not have both blood and chosen family and instead must settle for chosen family—chosen family who sometimes are also part of the violence. She shared fearing disposability, knowing that things we fear can be perceived even when they're not a reality.

I shared that I spent decades with that same fear. We sat with the fear until the sun rose. Now I am here sitting with a fear I no longer have, and a yearning to remember you, to forgive, to be grateful. To remember me and my journey, to forgive any parts of my journey that I may have been at odds with along the way, and the gratitude to everything that allowed my being here, held in community, by the sea, by the cliffs, and the mountains in the distance behind me.

To everyone who has harmed me 101

For years after you, I worked on building community and establishing transformative justice practices for similar situations to those I was impacted by. It started with inner-child work, an exploration of love ethics, and building community spaces to sit with the experiences and feelings.

In one such space, during an eclipse, I reflected on how in Arabic the word for forgiveness is "عفو" or "غَفَرَ." Both words mean "to pardon," and on a deeper level "to obliterate all traces." In English, the roots can be traced to Germanic words for "forward, forth." A couple of months later, it struck me that in Arabic the word we use to respond to thank you is "عفواً," which means "to forgive." Its second root means "wellness." We respond to gratitude with forgiveness, always.

I learned, in practice there are unlimited pathways for forgiveness. An ecosystem of interconnected systems feed and uplift one another. Without forgiveness we are not balanced, thus we are not healthy and well. When we move forgiveness away from accountability then we embrace and practice nonattachment.

At the time, this was the hardest thing I had ever had to do.

I meet with Ayman again that afternoon, and every day after for ten days, sometimes alone, sometimes within groups. As a spirit healer, I witness and walk alongside others on their journeys.

Today, we're in the sea, past the shallow end where the waves crash. We are on our backs, inhaling deeply, exhaling and inhaling quickly to allow our lungs to keep us afloat without any other movement. After years of this practice, I don't think about my breathing, mindful of Ayman's instead. Every inhale is a reminder that our bodies know. Our bodies

102   *Letters from a Living Utopia*

know how to float, even if we don't know how to swim. Our bodies know how to die, even if we do not feel prepared. Our bodies know how to release, even when we don't.

For millennia, people released and cleared together through dance, bathing, birthing, coming of age, death rituals, yoga, prayer, and so much more.

We eat lunch with one of the groups after, and I find myself reflecting on a different experience from 2017.

The organization I founded and was running at the time hosted the first SWANA Suicidality Summit in Jordan. During the summit, a researcher shared that Jordanian youth had the highest suicide rate in the region. For many, this was shocking. Jordan is surrounded by war and is in relative peace comparatively.

A few days later, I was meeting with an organizer from the West Bank and shared this, and she was not surprised at all. She shared that she hates being in Jordan because there are no pathways to support releasing and clearing emotions. In the West Bank, on the other hand, she said when someone is killed by the settler-colonial state, they all mourn together, and when someone gets married, they all celebrate regardless of who knows who.

Emotions are always expressed. In Jordan, as I lived through, you are often told you have it so much better than everyone else and to keep it inside. Keeping it inside is deadly.

As I watch the group interact, I am reminded that releasing and clearing are not only on a physical level. A release is in our bodies, minds, and our souls.

After the lunch, Ayman tells me she's ready.

That evening, Ayman is painted with henna, outlining her story and what she is releasing. Hours into the night, we

To everyone who has harmed me 103

form a dabke line around a bonfire. The smile on her face lights the sky, channeling the beginnings of a new moon.

Even now, I am grateful for the reminders, though I do not carry any of you with me and have not for decades. The ten-year anniversary of the revolution is on the horizon, and we are still healing. We will heal for all time, building worlds every day, a new beginning every moment.

I pray that you found your own new beginnings in this world, though I know that even in a liberated world there are those who are not ready for the liberation of others. Wherever you are, may you find where you are meant to be, whatever those paths look like for you. And if you do not, I know that your harm is irrelevant.

I turn to the sea to end the night, feeling the salty water seeping into my skin. I reflect on the memories stored in this sea, my people lost within it crystallized as the salt now surrounding me, uplifting me. I thank them for the abundance of this land and walk home, to be held by community, always.

Releasing in community,
From a memory claimed by the sea

LETTER ELEVEN
5/Scorpio/3

Dear Hawa & Rakan,

I want to say I was surprised to see your letter folded neatly in my mailbox the day before last, but I have been expecting it since the new moon and knew it was delayed at the post due to the storms we had last week.

You've been on my mind for twenty years, and although I expected the letter, my hands still shook as I opened the pink envelope and read and reread every word, as if there was a hidden meaning behind each.

I missed much of your upbringing. I held you days after you were born, the first in our family to do so. More than anyone else, I witnessed the first two years of your lives.

106 *Letters from a Living Utopia*

Then . . . It might be hard to explain, but at the time transphobia was being weaponized to move us toward fascism, and your parents accepted it, even as it was not in line with their values. I do not share this to create a wedge between you, nor do I say it with any emotion after all these years. We have all grown and continue to grow.

I saw you again once, in Jordan a couple of years later, and you looked at me like I was a stranger, as if I had abandoned you. In a way, I had. For that, I am sorry. I have been for decades.

I do not bring up these memories to sit in unhealed sorrow, for I believe we have all healed since our family's reunification and nothing I have written here is new to you. I share this to honor the shared loss we have all felt and to honor my own experiences of grieving you.

I share them to reflect on a new conflict in our family and the joy I receive in us moving through it together.

Years ago, I yearned for our family to heal and to be healed for a moment. I was tired of the violence, tired of threatening boundaries. You have probably heard that my relationship with the family was largely fear-based in the world we were born in. At the time, most people expected that I was afraid of the family, but ever since I was a child, it was the rest of the family that was always afraid of me. I was an autistic child who understood how people wielded power. I was terrifying to most. I am grateful that my values have always been liberatory for I would have been terrified of myself were I to abandon my principles.

At one point though, I was tired. This would have been about seventeen years ago, around your fourth birthday, when I decided that fear-based familial relationships are not what

Dear Hawa & Rakan 107

I yearn for, and I stepped away. This was years after cutting out your parents and consequently abandoning you in the process. I yearned for things to be fixed without me forcing them and I wanted an end to the violence. I wanted a sustainable relationship with your grandparents and aunts and you. I knew and wanted to forget that relationships are not sustainable. Not even utopia or liberation is sustainable.

Back then, *sustainment* had been at the forefront of my work for years. After all, transformation is just change if it is not sustainable. I came to this realization quite accidentally as I was writing an essay sometime before you were born. I searched for the Arabic word for "sustainable," to consider the full implications of its meanings. The word is "مستمر" which means "to continue, to keep moving." In English the word sustain is rooted in Old French, *sostenir* or *sustenir*, which means "to hold up, bear; suffer, endure."

The words that lit up for me were moving, suffer, and endure. When I say transformation is sustainable, does that imply that it must be able to continue moving, evolving even? Does it mean that suffering is in store and it must be endured?

"Endure," in particular, has always seemed to me to imply self-infliction in various connotations. It is synonymous with "to bear," but that implies a burden placed upon us without consent.

When leading meditations, I invite folks to bring forward the weight they are carrying on their shoulders that was never theirs to begin with. This reminds me of that. The ability to distinguish between the weight that was meant for us to carry and the weight that we should never have carried is a beautiful practice in self-awareness.

How much weight are we carrying that is not ours to carry as we work toward healthy relationships with one another? As we move toward transformation? As we continuously build liberated lives?

Decades into this work and I am still evolving, but evolution is not only creation and growth, it is also claiming and renewing knowledge and wisdom that we have always known. The "we" I speak of embraces all humanity and the inheritances that come from our ancestors, the land, and spirit.

For decades, I have asked myself, "How do transformation and utopia work if we are to remain nonattached? Is sustainability not at odds with nonattachment?"

I can feel something curious pushing the right side of my frontal lobe, trying to make its way through: contradictions, manifestations of intentionality, yearnings for sustainability, deviations, and so much else, taking space, demanding to be heard.

Transformation and utopia are not sustainable destinations, they are a balance of ongoing and maybe opposing forces. Suffering is not the antithesis to utopia. Suffering exists in utopia. Suffering exists within transformation.

Change is constant and moves in many directions simultaneously. Transformation therefore requires direction and intentionality, especially to become systemic, to manifest as a large-scale deviation from the norm form of change. Utopia is also intentional, built every day, reached every day, a constant amidst constant change.

I think back to being twenty years old and selling a twenty-year-old car, our destinies somehow seeming tied to our birth, separated by only a few months. This car, like the

Dear Hawa & Rakan 109

rest of me at the time, was often trying to kill me. In fact, this was going to be the final thing I did before leaving this plane of existence. I figured even a few hundred dollars would be nice to leave to my sisters.

After work, one evening in late June, I drove over to a house in a small town near where I was living at the time. A man wanted to purchase it for his eighteen-year-old daughter. He drove the car—he knew a lot more than I did about cars—and took some pictures to show to the daughter. He asked if I'd like to come inside as we waited for her to get back to him. He was Lebanese, so his invitation was more of a directive, and within minutes, I was inside his home, a platter of hummus and pita bread and who knows what else in front of me.

He spoke of home, of his journey, and within an instant, he had offered to host me during the next Eid, saying regardless of what happens with the car, that I had a home here away from home.

I was barely verbal those days, managing to say the few words here and there that I needed for my engineering job, or when police pointed guns at me following the Boston Marathon bombing.

I did not know how to explain that at that point in my life, I had never had a home, that home was a dream that did not exist in this plane. I did not know how to explain that I would be purging the hummus later because my body could not break it down anymore.

I do not know what he saw. I do not even know what I looked like those days, my body dysmorphia at an all-time high. What I saw were hollow dead eyes that preceded the rest of me, bones that were beyond aches, and malnutrition through homelessness and the pits of depression. I don't even know how long I was there. Was it ten minutes or two hours?

When I walked out of his home that day, I hated him so much. He had tied an anchor to my leg and moving between realms was so much harder than it had been moments before meeting him.

I do not know his name. He bought the car for $1,500 and we never spoke again. In that house, I glimpsed utopia. I do not know what their lives were like in that house or beyond it. I do not know if any of them felt what I felt there. It was a single moment, but everything changed.

As far as I know, he will never know the impact he had. Even if he read these words, he might not recognize the version of him I experienced. Perhaps he too is yearning for utopia. In an instant, he opened a gateway to utopia for me. As I write this, it has been almost thirty years since that moment. I wonder where he is, though I do not seek him out. I pray that he and everyone else find home.

I wanted to share this story of how I learned to move, even in the darkest moments of my life, through the portals of utopia wherever they open up, in relationships with others, with the land, with spirit, and with life itself.

Our family wants me "home," where they are. You ask for me to return as well. Family reunification can be beautiful, but I cannot return in this moment in time. I make this decision without malice or attachment to the past; in fact, it's the opposite. I love you all, but spirit has tasked me with a role here, a role that does not include our family.

Someday, we will be reunited, but until then I am called to a different path. I no longer expect a sustainable relation-

Dear Hawa & Rakan 111

ship before my return. I do not need us to manifest this return or be intentional as we walk around the sharp edges that still live within us in this new world that none of us know.

I am grateful for your letter and allowing me to ramble about these barely pieced-together reflections, for they have provided me with answers I did not fully realize I was open to receiving.

I am asking myself what happens if we live our lives in the most humane of ways. I know from my own experience the answer. Utopia happens. Perhaps we are at the precipice of making that happen on a larger scale than ever before, but what happens next is beyond all of us. Will we turn to humanity? Or will we turn our backs once again?

I stare at the rubble on this beach in Gaza as I write this. It has been over fifteen years since an amount of bombs equivalent to multiple nuclear attacks were dropped here. Most of it has been rebuilt, but not this small stretch of beach in the north. I watch the Mediterranean reach out, the sea calmly moving toward me instead of its usual waves that crash into the soft sand. There's no one else here as I reflect. For the last few years, I have been able to collaborate with so many who were part of the revolutions and all the care that existed within it. It is nice to be alone with my thoughts for a minute before returning to town to care for others as we rebuild, as we evolve, as we suffer, and we endure. I do all this ecstatically of course. I am still tired today, but not how I was all those years ago, and instead of wanting it all to be "fixed," I am excited to move through this process with others, as we claim this new world.

I was wrong, as is often the case as I work through things for myself before sharing them to the world. Utopia *is* sustain-

112 *Letters from a Living Utopia*

able, but not in the way that I had grown accustomed to using that word. Utopia is not a destination that will be difficult to take away from us once it is there. Utopia is constant motion, it includes enduring and suffering, and it exists both within and beyond our perceptions of intentions.

We are here, and we find each other, in this constant motion. I will always love you and you, and I will always be evolving separately, just as you evolve separately, and evolving with and without the entire family. I love you. We all love you as we know you love us. Conflict is a pathway of love and a deepening of that evolution, not a denial of it. I am grateful for the reminders you inspired within me during our last conversation.

Constantly moving to loving you,
Yaffa

LETTER TWELVE
25/Gemini/22

Dear Beloved Language,

On the twentieth anniversary of the launch of the Center for Language Expansion and Reclamation, I write you this reflection to express my gratitude and love for all that you grant us daily. To be honest, the idea to write you came to me as an afterthought, for I was tasked with compiling letters I have written throughout the years since liberation, and I found it only fitting to include one specific to you.

I have not always cared for language and etymology. My mother tongue is Arabic, but between immense dissociation and selective mutism from autism, I do not remember words

114   *Letters from a Living Utopia*

before being six and moving to what was then known as Arizona from Jordan, when I began to learn English.

It took me a couple of years to learn the language. I could understand spoken Arabic and English but speaking myself was a challenge for some time, well into my teens for English and early twenties for Arabic.

My autistic brain did not like English. So much of it did not make sense to me. It took me four years to understand what everyone around me was saying about "their," "there," and "they're." It took me years to understand that the sun had a gendered counterpart in "son."

Arabic, you were different. I was thrown into an Arabic school as a freshman in high school in Jordan with a writing and reading comprehension level of a six year old. I did not show up most days, so it was fine until senior year.

By that time, the Arabic teacher at the boys' school hated me, so my parents got me the girls' teacher as a tutor. I would later learn she was homophobic and transphobic and a multitude of other things, but she charmed me with the language nonetheless. She broke it down and I fell in love with the mother tongue I once knew but forgot.

I love how every word can be broken down into a three-letter root. From the root, you can understand everything. Not just definitions but also motivations. The history of words is inscribed within them. I adore your simplicity and complexity. Every letter is a building block for endless worlds.

The first letter in my birth name is Alif, the letter of all creation. The first letter in my name is Ya', the final letter in the alphabet representing death in its most beautiful forms. I learned magic through those letters. Finally, something made sense.

Dear Beloved Language 115

I ended up with the highest grade in my class.

Then things changed, and I guess they had been changing for a year prior. Language did not save me sleeping on park benches during that year and after. Language, like most things, was forgotten in the process of survival. But words helped. It was one hundred thousand words that got me accepted into an engineering school. It was words that put me on stages to talk about mental health, anti-patriarchy, and sexual assault prevention. Words became part of the fabric of who I am to survive. The very first workshop I ever ran was about the power of words.

However, in the years before the dawn of liberation, I had grown frustrated with words. Words were disloyal, easily hijacked, and in English they do not resist. For example, at the time the word "transformation" had gone from a word rarely spoken, that left rooms quaking, to an adjective used endlessly and meaninglessly. "Equity" used to raise eyebrows. "Justice" meant something.

In a matter of years, these words would become meaningless, weaponized to immobilize us as the colonial project advanced.

I grew frustrated with constantly having to find the next word, making movement spaces more elitist and less accessible.

The first transformative justice learning workshop I ran was about the elitism of words. It had struck me that the most marginalized of the most marginalized are usually the ones who do not have words to speak their experiences.

Often, we are not permitted into spaces about us. I did not have language for transness until my mid-twenties. I was barred from spaces that claimed to represent me by white cis people who knew words describing white experience that never applied to me.

I have stopped working to move beyond words. Instead, I focus on claiming language and have been doing so for over three decades.

Etymology is rooted in history. For the last two decades, in this post-liberation world, we have been reclaiming language while acknowledging etymology. I went from using utopia as a concept to liberation and ultimately, moving toward the language of nature. We were born to be liberated; it is natural. Anything unnatural now describes things that move us away from liberation. That wasn't the case in the world I grew up in. Nature was code for fascism and eugenics.

I am here for rebranding and reclaiming, but that does not work without acknowledging the etymology.

Rebranding a definition that never existed in the first place except in collective societal memory is not as impactful as recognizing the root of words and original meanings and building new pathways. Nature was never meant to be weaponized by fascism, and neither were we.

I still remember a call I had in 2023 with a participant in one of my fellowship programs. The incredible participant mentioned how she is always strength-focused and tries to move away from weakness. I learned to be careful in how I bring etymology into spaces. If words are working for individuals, who am I to deny that? However, like in this situation, folks are often frustrated because something that they are told is right is not working. There is a gap and misalignment somewhere.

I shared that etymologically, weakness means "to bend" and strength means "fort." I suggested that sometimes, in

Dear Beloved Language 117

fact, we grow through weakness, while we barricade and become immobile through strength. It was what we both needed at the time. Saying these words out loud cemented this reality for me.

I feel fortunate that the spaces I've been in over the last twenty years are grounded in the etymology of words. It has been a long journey, from learning to ask what words meant to people in peer support practice, to defining everything, to now allowing etymology to do the heavy lifting to support spaces in maintaining "natural" realities.

Twenty years ago, I started this journey on the precipice of liberation. It started out with simple searches for language and moved into working with etymologists as we began living utopia daily. I had never thought of etymologists as world-builders, but in that era, we catalyzed our imagination and we began building space through a new orientation to language.

It was such a blessing having space in Arabic to map history and strategize on how to live and breathe utopia, through the language within ourselves, shared in groups, and beyond that.

We were able to build together thanks to you. May you always describe our futures and carry our pasts, with us, for us.

Forever,
Yaffa

LETTER THIRTEEN
2/Taurus/25

Dear Mama,

I visit you like I do every week where your body was once buried, and although I know there is nothing left of the body you wore, I visit anyway because the memories of you that I have invested on my visits still are. I dreamt I said goodbye to you last night, in a world I had thought no longer occupied any part of my mind.

The dream reminded me of words published decades ago in one of my earliest works called *sage.*

Letters from a Living Utopia

Entrapped

I had a dream

the FBI only
entraps us
when we are accepted
by our families

Trans folks are
the most threatening
when loved

so I had to say
goodbye to mama
to pretend
we were estranged

the FBI left
I left
never to see her
again

The smell of jasmine reminds me of my childhood in Sweileh. Do you remember it? We probably remember it very differently, me a child running away and you newly displaced—your mom dies, birth after birth, car robbery, then we leave. You were still in your twenties. My twenties were filled with homelessness and other forms of violence, yet I will never know what it's like to care for five children through it.

Do you remember what you used to tell us though? In between food stamp lines, times when you told us to play until the food was ready knowing that there was no food. You used to tell us that we were rich, that we came from palaces,

Dear Mama 121

that richness was not about the material. I remembered your words as I was unhoused across multiple continents, as others around me betrayed their values just to get a little bit further ahead in the fucked-up game of capitalism. I learned from you that there is no money that can buy our values. It wasn't that you were telling us to be rich, you were telling us that it is not the material that matters; rather it is the spiritual and how we connect with one another.

You know, once upon a time I hated you. It wasn't because of the harm that you had caused, for I didn't understand harm back then. I hated the vision you had, and in my teenage years, I did not want to know that things would get better. There was too much loss, too much violence. I think I stopped hating you after you said the worst thing you had ever said to me, because then you had betrayed that vision, and we could all be miserable together.

You were the first to teach me about vision and belief systems that transcend us. You taught me that a shared vision matters because it guides and inspires us. I fought against this for years.

Then I started to learn beyond you.

I was unhoused as the Syrian revolution began, unhoused between borders, the sound of bombs in the distance, friends disappearing for having the vision and courage to fight. I was there when the first of the Syrians came through, believing they would be home by the end of the week, the vacation that Palestinians believed in decades prior. They would not go back home for fifteen years, just like we did not go home for one hundred. But that didn't matter, just like it didn't matter that we no longer lived in palaces on our land, what mattered was how we showed up.

122   *Letters from a Living Utopia*

I learned community care that year, my own pain invisible, shedding weight as if I was allergic to my own muscle mass. As I moved across oceans, I learned that across different crises the vision ought to be the same. But it wasn't . . . It took me a while to realize this, that just because a person is showing up for social justice does not mean they are here for liberation. I learned utopia is rarely the vision at all, most believing it's impossible and even more not wanting it, uncomfortable with what they will no longer have.

By my mid-twenties, I had moved much of my organizing to building alternative systems, and toward the end of 2019, I yearned to build a space for frontline organizers to come together to envision a decade or two into the future. At the time, we were always behind the systems of oppression surgically shredding our souls, and I wanted to ask the question of what they will do to us next, and next, and next. What we would build to address these things ten years from now instead of waiting for it to come to us first.

The summit was scheduled for March 2020.

I didn't make it, if you remember. I was home with you in Jordan as the borders closed, and as they did. I closed the door of my high school room and did not see anyone until June. The summit did not happen. The summit that was meant to bring us together to discuss the rise of pandemics, surveillance, AI, the wrath of empire as it falls, was canceled due to the start of a pandemic.

In hindsight, organizing during those first few months of the COVID-19 pandemic, though unprecedented, was the easiest organizing I had ever done. Mutual aid came naturally to me and in all the places others usually resisted liberation,

Dear Mama 123

they were willing to sit back and do the work. It is easier for some to have a shared vision, even temporarily, when the world is crashing down.

But our minds are adaptable, and the world crashing down becomes the norm, like our bodies adjusting to the speed as we freefall, making it seem as if we are floating instead of coming crashing down. Then we pretend as if we're not all heading down to the same destination, as if we have a choice in whether or not liberation will happen, as if we will be safe without a parachute and that we're not all going to crash sooner rather than later unless we take action. Some will release parachutes to delay the inevitable, while others will think you're the problem for telling the truth and turn away as you freefall.

Conflict tends to arise three to six months into a crisis. Then, six to nine months in, things begin tearing apart and, all of a sudden, we don't realize that we're all falling together.

The same thing happened after October 7, 2023. Do you remember? Do you remember our conversation on your birthday? Do you remember the conversation several days later when I was the one who had to tell you about your dead family members?

The same thing happened. Three months later, it was increasingly normal. So normal. Nine months into it, I no longer knew what was left of the movement.

But here is the thing. I have always lived with hope. I have always lived with a vision of liberation and utopia. I have always known these things are not dependent on me or a single person, we are heading toward liberation whether we want to or not.

124   *Letters from a Living Utopia*

To hold a vision of liberation is an intimate thing. To step into a space with yourself or others and dream is one of the most intimate things you can ever do. Remember when you shared your vision for utopia? It was as the student encampments were growing. You said if they can rise up, then Falasteen will be free. What you did not know is that I was part of the movement, supporting the community as we navigated conflict, as we built skills, as we struggled.

I wish I could have shared more of my work with you back then. I would have loved your thoughts and wisdom, but oceans stood between us and by the time we spoke, my work had shifted. Those days were like the tides rising from a new hurricane veering toward the coast. You also knew that this work put me at risk and there was no good any of us could do that was worth your child's life. You have always known that I had to give my life for liberation, and I know that was not easy to accept and overlook. It almost felt like you resented liberation because you knew I was to be sacrificed in the process. In reality, it was our relationship that was sacrificed, strangers made of the same blood, no ill will between them but a war to be fought on different grounds that keep them apart for a lifetime.

But I became who I am because of you. You taught me to vision-build and like any healthy child, I made it my own, did the work I was meant to beyond you, and even brought lessons back to you.

For ten years prior to October 7th, I watched you be accountable and grow far beyond what society at the time thought possible. I sat with you at twenty, as you shared the neighbors' problems and I shared about post-partum depression and your eyes opened wide as you asked if depression is

Dear Mama 125

what I had been talking about for years, and I said yes, and you asked why I never said anything. It hit you without a need to respond and you did better the next day and the day after. We built a relationship through your accountability.

Little by little, you learned to apologize, to acknowledge harm, to communicate your needs with others, to own your life.

When you visited me a few months after October 7th, you asked where I kept my strainer, and I said I didn't know because someone was staying in my house while I was away. You were shocked to learn I didn't know who they were, that my house was routinely used for solidarity housing for people in emergencies I didn't know and would likely never meet.

It was a beautiful moment for me, because at that moment I reminded you of what community care looks like. It's funny, because I saw you do the same when I was a child. We learn and we forget and sometimes it's people we have taught who remind us of who we really are. None of us can ever do this alone.

Around the one-year anniversary of the start of the genocide in Gaza and the West Bank, I realized we had to overcome our fear of heights and look down, realizing utopia is ours and will always be ours. I realized that to build vision, we just need to remember the world we are heading toward regardless of all obstacles, tragedies, and setbacks.

I witnessed what's possible with you and you inspired me to build alternative systems that allow us to live out utopia instead of waiting for it to crash into us. We realized then that we cannot lead liberated lives without the proper infrastructure. This infrastructure must be holistic, inclusive of resources, skill-building, leadership development, conflict

126   *Letters from a Living Utopia*

transformation and accountability, and to our eyes back then, that looked a lot like transformative and disability justice.

You don't fully know this, but in late 2016, my PTSD was retriggered, the accumulation of the toxicity of the United States presidential election cycle, the violence within the nonprofit industrial complex, and the disposability that exists within it.

For months all I had was rage that nearly consumed me. I bought *Killing Rage* because I assumed bell hooks was going to help me eliminate my rage. I carried the book with me wherever I traveled, but I never had the space to read it.

Finally, in May 2017, I found myself in three different hospitals following a near-death experience by suicide. At McLean hospital, it took a couple of days to realize the individuals there, as well-meaning as they were, were not going to be able to help me.

At the time, my most pressing mental health concern was that I loved and appreciated myself too much to live in a world filled with such severe injustice. I wanted and deserved more.

At the hospital though, they looked at mental health challenges as consequences to addictive behavior or issues of self-esteem. They placed me within the self-esteem group. I tried explaining my reasoning to the various staff members. It was during the following day that I started reading *Killing Rage*. It was the only book I had with me, and I felt transformed from the very first line: "I am writing this essay sitting beside an anonymous white male that I long to murder."

Such powerful words, such immense validation, and immediately I learned that my rage too was valid. I learned that rage was not what I had been taught, that it was not a

Dear Mama 127

tool of destruction, to be hidden and prevented at all cost. Rage can be beautiful, it is valid, and it exists within every single one of us after injustice. And it is through this rage that we can build a better world and dream of utopia.

It is with this rage that I had done *all* the work I had done.

Everything I have built I built with my rage and the rage of my people. And that is beautiful. It was in that moment that I moved beyond the internalized stigma I carried for being a displaced, disabled, queer, trans Muslim. I always tried to make myself small to not fall into the terrorist stereotype. As a Muslim and at the time male-passing person, I was taught in the Western world that terrorism was my legacy, and any anger, let alone rage, will be seen as terrorism.

I learned that I am valid, that all emotions are valid, and that a better world will not be created by denying parts of who I am and limiting my possibilities. Utopia has unlimited possibilities, and I could not build that world or envision it.

Reclaiming rage allowed me to reclaim our relationship, for your rage was always iconic. Your rage growing up was misdirected, and it wasn't until later that you learned to direct it where it was meant. I learned what I needed to know about my rage through you and bell hooks during those years. Sometimes we learn by being offered a healthy example, sometimes the opposite.

I also learned about vision, accountability, and the power of contradiction from you.

Our relationship has always been contradictory, like most parent-child relationships at the edges of war and displacement. In many ways, I have never been your child. I was grocery shopping alone by the age of seven, and you would pick me up from a curb with a dozen bags weighing more than my body would for years to come. Your emotions were explosive, releasing memories at the same time. I held your emotions and remembered every harm anyone has ever caused you. I remembered for the both of us. At one point you realized that I was not a child. We carried this into adulthood, mine at least. You were twenty-five when you birthed me, but I have always been older.

We were a contradiction.

The year before the start of the final revolution, on a call with a dear friend discussing the beginning of Saturn's return, he shared the feelings of being stuck in contradiction. I found myself saying, perhaps for the first or thousandth time, that our contradictions are the birthplaces of transformation.

Contradiction is a particular type of chaos that we are told is threatening. That should be our first clue, as most things deemed threatening by the system hold unruly and transformative potential.

Contradictions also exist because systemic oppression utilizes them to stabilize itself, stave off crisis, and subjugate us.

Instead of using these contradictions for transformative liberation, they were used to gaslight the most marginalized. Contradictions were the basis for the medical industrial complex, prison industrial complex, and all other systems that upheld oppression for nearly six hundred years. But there is power in contradiction, something systems of oppression capitalized on.

Contradictions extend beyond time and space. Creation in every form is a contradiction whether you believe in a higher power, science, and/or nothing at all.

Dear Mama 129

I wonder what word you would have used here, for I don't think it would have been "contradiction." That is valid and wonderful! Language has the power we give it.

Nonattachment is birthed through contradictions. I can take action and have no control of the outcome is a contraction, and it is transformative.

Holding and honoring multiple contradictory truths at the same time requires immense value system change, which is the basis of transformation.

Sufi Muslims believe that Allah is found where opposites meet. Without contradictions and the unknown, there would be no Gods, myths, folklore, or any stories that we tell ourselves to make sense of the things that seemingly do not make sense. The greatest power exists in this space. The world is transformed and remade again and again through stories that aim to fill this unknown. The person who can fill it is the most powerful person on Earth.

Power comes from claiming these contradictions every day. Recognizing that you can still love someone who is trying to kill you and still be nowhere near them. Recognizing nonduality, moving beyond attachment, is all about claiming contradiction. Claiming contradiction equitably is not filling the gaps to control others; that is abuse. Claiming contradiction equitably is surrendering to the unknown, savoring it, and using it to open more space for folks in the margins of marginalization, those in the margins of contradiction.

Those of us who were in the margins lived in our own contradictions, like the two of us. We did not make sense to those solidly placed in the known. But claiming contradiction is part of what it takes to recognize everyone and regard everything as valid. Spaces of belonging cannot be created outside of contradiction. Now, we can embrace those to a point where they're no longer contradictions. In our liberation, we all have power and we all embrace power.

I am grateful for all I learned from you. And I am sorry for the weight you carried witnessing the consequences of my implementation of those lessons.

I have known about the consequences of organizing in equitable and transformative ways my entire life. Over the years, my assessment of how deeply rooted that violence is has only expanded.

Dreaming was threatening. This work was threatening.

To imperialism, any vision of a world of egalitarian, decolonial justice, any utopia imagined by a Muslim, is terrorism.

Back then, vision-building for utopia was uncomfortable, and depending on who you ask, it could either be filled with liberation or more oppression. This is why I exclusively centered voices of folks in the margins of marginalization and contradiction. We now live in the world built from the margins in, not from the center out.

I want to close this letter with one final memory. I am six, it is Ramadan, and I wake up late for *suhoor* on a Saturday morning. The sun is shining brightly in the living room of the cricket house. You are awake. I'm not entirely sure why, but I think you might be mad at me for not waking up. Instead, you smile at me, one of the few times you ever do during my childhood. You wrap me in a blanket and you make me breakfast. This is the best meal of my life, liberation or not. There will never be a better memory. It is the best in a lifetime of beautiful memories filled with a life lived ecstatically and utopically.

Dear Mama 131

I miss you and I will always love you.

The six year old still wrapped in a blanket of your love,
Yaffa

LETTER FOURTEEN
23/Scorpio/32

Dear Death,   •

I feel you resting upon my body like a thobe after harvest, my skin and mind attached by the lightness of sweat and life. I feel the heat tethering us and know even if I were to try to take you off you would cling to my skin and make this awkward for everyone. But I do not want to take you off, nor have I ever. As I prepare for your full arrival, bathing, washing my body in orange rose oil, lighting an olive oil candle, resting on my favorite pillow and surrounded by my loved ones I am reminded of pleasure.

I still smile at the thought that this death ritual seems so sexual in so many ways. I remember decades ago, talking to a birthday twin, someone I did not know twenty-four hours earlier, about sex. I say, "Sex is not about pleasure. To say sex is about pleasure is to deny that pleasure is a constant. Every moment of every day can be filled with pleasure. This does not deny or erase pain, for pain is also pleasure."

But I also say, "Sex is so deep of a connection that you disappear, melding with one or more others, and feel one with the universe and all life."

She smiled and said, "Yeah, sex doesn't do that for me." We both laughed as one does when "bad" sex used to come up. What a different world, where sex was not easily talked about. Sex was not a skill that we developed, it was a shameful thing you hid away underneath blankets and in the dark.

I don't want to think about that world right now, but I do, and instead of thinking of bad sex, I think of Audre Lorde and her wisdom around the power of the erotic.

The erotic is life. Life is pleasure. The erotic is pleasure. It is not, and has never been, about sex.

I think she would have enjoyed this world I have lived in and am dying in, where every relationship feels like a connection with every part of the universe.

Our erotic philosophy now allows us to recognize the vastness of the possibility we had not been claiming. Sure, you can experience orgasm during sex, but why not orgasm hundreds of times a day (orgasm is not synonymous with ejaculation like it used to be)?

I have not served as a birthing doula in decades. Once liberation was achieved, I found myself called to the spiritual healing that exists past our first breath. But for years prior, I saw the immense difference support achieves for bringing

Dear Death 135

humans into this world. Orgasmic births seemed like an impossibility, but they weren't.

It is absolutely incredible what we can do to be with our bodies and to find pleasure in bringing life into this world. This applies far before a child is born, during, and after—regardless of who carries the baby.

For millennia, we raised children communally. As we got rid of community structures, we had also made birthing and childcare excruciating for everyone involved. But when I worked with birthers, they were able to maintain healthy practices and have their needs met by building communal structures of care around them. Today, this is common.

I have never birthed a child in this life, but I have raised many, and it was always in community. For years, it had fascinated me that individuals were not willing to do the community-building work as they considered bringing another human into this world. We know part of it was the education in that world, but more than that it was the lack of responsibility for our being. We are meant to be collectivist, every decision based in community. There is no individual.

I remember this as I remember you because this was a form of death that the vast majority of the people born with me had to contend with. Death of the ego on one hand, and death of everything else we had known.

Life and death have always overlapped for me, extensions of themselves, dressed only in different gowns. I claimed one to move toward the other. Surviving capitalism was hard, but the death that was needed to unlearn it was not.

I have been close to you my entire life, and my proximity was material and deeply felt since I was seventeen. Between seventeen and twenty-six, death was around every corner, under every bed, in every window. Death was everywhere. I was thirty-one during the conversation I described above. I turned thirty-two in a still colonized Falasteen, and now I am ageless. Even now, preparing for you, I do not know if this is my last year in this energy form. I think the fact that no one knows is brilliant.

You are not a shadow I move toward. You are not a shadow I move away from. Death is there, it is constant, it will happen when it happens. I will be claimed when I am meant to be.

I have been asked over the years how the dying process has changed after liberation. I often say that death is a utopic practice that extends beyond external liberation. For years, I had supported individuals on their journeys to you as a doula, and the journey itself did not change when I was working with them. Claiming death is one of the most powerful things. Claiming death was a pathway to claiming liberation before the rest of the world had caught up. Death was utopic in an unliberated world. During those years, I learned to not only claim you as utopic, but to claim you as pleasure.

I am enamored by how our bodies will birth completely new cells every seven years. I have felt pleasure as my body has become more disabled with age. I feel pleasure in feelings of oneness with the world. Everything dies. Everything, from the largest to the smallest of things.

What did change is what happened after death and how people died. No more genocide, no more paperwork that bankrupts you to bury your family.

Death makes a lot of people feel inconsequential, and instead of dreading that, I love it. The world will not end with me. It will end with someone one day, or more accurately,

Dear Death 137

humanity will end with someone. I do not think that will be me, and even if it was, it is just death after all.

Saying I revere death was a cause for concern in most spaces back then. However, when I became a certified death doula I could say, "As a death doula, I revere death," and it was much more accepted. It is silly how we created boundaries to pleasure and joy. Everything is filled with pleasure, even death. Pleasure is not the antithesis to pain; it is not a denial. I can grieve and experience pleasure at the same time.

Pleasure is a chemical response from our nervous and hormonal systems. It is not dependent on any one event. We are capable of experiencing it during the worst and best of events. We are capable of experiencing it always. It's the judgment from society claiming morality that limited our possibilities.

I have lived an erotic life, from birth, to witnessing Teta pass at the cusp of two, to running for the first time both away and toward, painting for the first time, writing my first novel, my second, the third, finding my voice, supporting others in finding their voice, engaging in community care and mutual aid, grieving loved ones lost to settler colonialism and then the revolution, every tree planted after, every person I worked with after, every day beyond that like I had every day before.

The Arabic word for erotic is "شهوان"—a word that has recently crept back into everyday life. The root is "شهو," which is the same word for hunger or tasty for food. In English, the root comes from the Greek word *erotikos*, which translates to "caused by passionate love, referring to love" and *érōs*, to "love, desire."

The erotic has not always meant the sexual or even the sensual. The erotic is a hunger, beyond our physical being.

To define the erotic as only in the context of a bodily desire is to deny that we are beings beyond our bodies and minds.

I believe this body is borrowed for our use in this lifetime. This body, glorious in its perfection, is created from stardust and all the minerals that make us tissues, bones, blood, and skin. This body is recycled to and from an ecosystem in the ground and in the sky. This body has been countless others and will be countless others beyond my existence within it. Just as it's impossible to own the land, one cannot have ownership in the body that carries them.

I struggled with this concept. As a Muslim, this was part of my upbringing. As an indigenous Palestinian, this is part of our practice. We belong to the land, and we return to it after dying. This body is not mine, my family's, or anybody else's.

I grew up with this concept, but when a similar concept was shared in yoga teacher training, I really struggled with it.

For years, I had focused on healing my mind. Two hundred hours of yoga training in twenty-one days was my investment in my body. I was there to connect with my body. That was the purpose. And on day two, they told me to practice a meditation that literally breathes in "I am not my body" and exhales "I am not my mind."

I practiced it and felt like I was abandoning my body. It felt as if my body was my inner child and I was shunning them, telling them they are not enough. About a week into the training, my body and mind were the ones who guided me. *Why would we pretend we are something we are not?* they asked during a meditation, shocking me into submission. *We are gifts*, they expressed through emotions and sensations far beyond words that ran through me. *We are not yours, and you are not ours.* In a way, they were telling me that I was trying

Dear Death 139

to claim something that was never mine in the first place and forcing them to fit the narrow box society had conditioned me to frame for them.

In Islam, we bury the dead immediately, because this body is not ours and it belongs to the land and must be returned. There is no embalming, no coffins or inhumane things that try to preserve something that was never ours to begin with. I will be buried within hours of our union, this body left behind as I return home with you.

Similarly, our minds are not ours. I am a being that exists within the larger context of the universe. I have never had an original thought or idea or creation. I am part of a universal conscience that I do not get to claim. I am brilliant, but that brilliance is not mine. I am powerful, but that power is not mine. Everything I build and create is from the universe and belongs to the universe.

I am part of the universe. That is not a mind or a body.

As a part of the universe, the erotic, then, is a hunger beyond bodies and minds. The erotic is a hunger for reunification with universal consciousness beyond the things that we pretend belong to us.

Tantra, Kundalini, samadhi, Jannah, and so many other concepts that dot the circle of time are always about unity with universal consciousness. Our bodies and minds can be a part of that story, but they are not the story. Our bodies and minds do not join us in universal consciousness. We are beyond anything owned or borrowed.

I use the word reunification intentionally here. We are returning to something, not finding it for the first time.

We already are the universe, but most of us have just forgotten. We forget that pure ecstasy is built within our fabric. We forget the erotic is not about sex and the greatest orgasms are when we are home in the universe. The erotic is beyond any and all identity and concepts we created to live in these bodies and minds. Home is not ancestral land because that land was never "mine" to begin with. I belong to the land, yet my being is beyond land.

I await you, my dear, on land that is not mine, in a utopia that does not belong to me or anyone else. I am and have always been in utopia. Embracing the erotic is embracing utopia. Even in a liberated society, there is no utopia without the erotic.

Awaiting our reunion,
Yaffa

LETTER FIFTEEN
3/Capricorn/33

Dear Yaffa,

I am uncovering letters I had written to myself over the years, and I found one from before we had liberation that was meant to be the start of a book about utopia. I smile writing this to you now, for you are the one who has been on this journey with me, before and since liberation, and in the moments in between where living and striving for liberation was a lonely undertaking.

Do you remember the first five years of life in Jordan, growing up in Arizona, Canada, and high school back in Jordan? Do you remember becoming an adult on the streets of Irbid, sleeping on park benches and wherever available?

Do you remember the start of the Syrian revolution, supporting Z and watching as his entire family perished? Do you remember the months of starvation? I have healed so much over the decades, yet starvation is not something I will ever move past. My body still clenches at the thought.

I don't bring this up to relive memories that I have learned from and moved past, I bring them up to validate that I came into adulthood on the border of the Syrian revolution, between continents, before finally finding you.

Mama and Baba grew up in Kuwait, displaced time and again. I wasn't any different than them. Constantly displaced, starting in Jordan, then Arizona, Canada, Jordan again, Syria, Turtle Island, Switzerland, Turtle Island again and again, Hong Kong, Malaysia, Turkey, Eire, Turtle Island, and eventually home.

I wrote words on my first visit to you, a place neither of us had been to at the time. Over sixty years of being barred from entering home. I spent thirty-two more than I should, but to imagine sixty and sixty-two is beyond me.

For thirty-two years, my positionality was as a settler on stolen land barred from ever returning to you.

At the time of my earlier writing and worldbuilding, I was a displaced Indigenous person who was not a Global North citizen, always at risk of being thrown to the next place, tossed around as the world tried to decide who could put up with us. I was exhausted.

Then, as fate would have it, I found my way back to Falasteen, momentarily, and I was no longer an Indigenous person who could not die on my land. I did not walk away willingly after that, but my sense of indigeneity was different.

Dear Yaffa 143

I found some of my writing from those years, and I wrote the following a year before I received my US citizenship:

> *I am also not of the Global North. Although many of these Global North countries are a part of my story, I am not a citizen, nor do I have a desire to assimilate and assemble within any of them. I will, however, accept citizenship when I am finally able to. Denying access to power is a form of abuse and it is disingenuous and harmful to sit wholly inside the rigid categories of citizenship or non-citizenship when our freedom and self-determination has always lived elsewhere, in our right to return to Falasteen.*

It's interesting how back then we had to always think of assimilation and assembly. We were in tidal waves of systems of oppression, always moving us one way or another, a minefield of pain and harm.

At the time, I assembled within Indigeneity, even before most Palestinians claimed theirs and for years after as many more realized it was tied to land stewardship and responsibility to community. Indigeneity is not only coming from a land, but about understanding our non-extractive relationship and responsibility that comes from being from a place.

I assembled with my agrarian and sweet-making Palestinian heritage that still remembered our Egyptian, Sudanese, Ethiopian, and Armenian roots. I assembled within a time where mutual aid and communal support did not need to be named as separate political commitments. A time before land ownership and supremacist individualism.

I assembled with Mama's side as freedom fighters, generations who faced the British and Zionists, and where there was almost no one left from the immediate family except for my grandfather.

I am of Falasteen, I will always be a steward of this land and caretaker of the community, and yet in the world I live in today, it hardly needs distinction. I assemble with the land now, we all do. To be liberated is to be one with the land and spirit.

I learned about utopia first through Teta, Mama's mom. I was twenty-two months old, and she was dying in the room behind me. Everyone was on edge, there were tears, and I too was crying when my uncle threatened me to stay quiet. I remember the ceiling was gray, and in my mind, Teta is wearing a red dress, still alive, a sense of peace not constrained by life and death surrounds her. I do not remember much beyond this vision. I struggle to remember the tubes, the medical equipment, the hospital bed, but mostly, she is in a red dress, solemn and at peace.

Death has never been something those around me feared. It is in death that my people spoke of utopia.

As a people who were colonized for thousands of years prior to white imperialism we have known death is not an end. A land inhabited by Canaanites and Nabateans for millennia prior. A land colonized as Egyptian, Greek, Judea, Persian, Roman, Arab-Muslim, Catholic, Arab-Muslim again, Catholic again, Ottoman, British, and Zionist.

My land knew blood for at least one hundred generations and three thousand years. My soul felt the weight of this history as it yearned for an end to white supremacist imperialism and settler colonialism. Today, I feel the weight of liberation, perfectly balanced across my body, mind, spirit, through the land, and throughout the community around me.

Dear Yaffa 145

What a journey this lifetime has been.

I walk into a masjid for Maghreb, and the sun is setting off the coast. Years ago, I thought I would be back home to you, but instead I found home up the coast in a smaller town, the swell of the Mediterranean calling me.

This masjid is like all I have witnessed the last several years since Falasteen has been liberated. Various spiritual practitioners use the space, for prayer we stand side by side; the borders of gender were forgotten years ago, individualized spiritual practice gone.

I pray and afterwards, my thoughts drift back to a time when my invisibility and hypervisibility as a Muslim and trans person impacted how I flowed through the world. It was in a masjid like this one where I write this letter that I moved deeper into utopia.

Between the way Mama and Baba spoke, and how my teachers spoke about liberation, I knew utopia was a moment away. Farther down the street from the masjid where we organized, I held onto the unshakable realization that not only was a better world so close, it was guaranteed, in every way, and if we died before we were fully liberated, still we were liberated as our bodies were returned into the ground. I yearned to be part of that liberation.

Those were the years I felt the most liberated, but not because I was a child, for I was never a child. Children are not meant to witness their mosque vandalized, to be interrogated by the FBI at the age of nine, experience housing vulnerability and all other kinds of insecurity, or watch their Mama take another job to pay for a medical procedure. I did not have a childhood, but I felt liberated in my understanding of the world, in being held in community, even as they came for us.

146 *Letters from a Living Utopia*

I learned that liberation is not dependent on systems of oppression; they influence the conditions from which liberation emerge, but liberation and oppression are opposites. The difference today is that there is no longer anyone coming for us.

Communities are built and then they blow away like the white fluff of a dandelion, building other communities wherever they land. We are always in community, always growing and expanding all that we are.

I think that's why I wanted to write this letter to you. I would like to explain why I never came back home. Walking along your streets for the first time felt like an astral projection. At the time I could not weep publicly or privately, years of genocide holding my tears hostage. I witnessed my family history written on your city walls and then lost for seventy-six years, and you asked me to bring that history back, return it where it was meant to be.

At the time, the North and Gaza were aflame, world wars looming, the fall of the empire imminent, and here I was, where it all started and . . . I could have come home, but you didn't need me like some of the others did. I have and will always love you, but I am of community, and you demand of me to be of community. I lived nearby first supporting children and adults. Then was called to Nasra to help build community care, to move past the organized crime that the Zionist government used to fracture Palestinians. I moved to Gaza to help with death and grief work. Then, I . . . well, you know the rest. Somehow, it still feels important to explain myself. My entire life, my heart has been fractured, pulled in different directions, and it's from the innermost abysses of the fracture that our utopia rose to the surface.

Dear Yaffa 147

For over a decade prior, I lived the life I thought I would live at home. You taught me utopia. I knew I would be a spirit healer living at home, I could smell the trees and the freshly baked bread. I could see the smiles of my loved ones at dinner and for years even before walking along your walls, I built that life. I became a spirit healer, mixing art, birthing, death, and peer support work.

I stand at the tip of the cliff as I write these words. I am grateful to everything that you are, for you are the largest piece in my heart that builds utopia. As long as you were in my heart, utopia was there, no matter the violence and oppression arrayed against us.

I know tonight will be my last night, dying at an age I never thought I would reach. On the precipice of the beyond, I can smell your streets like Teta used to as a child, your orange orchards that Seedo grew up on. After such a long journey, miraculous and heartbreaking, I am ready to come home, Teta's hands reaching out for mine.

From Yaffa to Yaffa,
Home

About the Author

Mx. Yaffa (they/she) is a trans Muslim displaced indigenous Palestinian culture worker and organizer. Their writings probe the yearning for home, belonging, mental health, queerness, transness, and other dimensions of marginalization while nurturing dreams of utopia against the background of ongoing displacement and genocide of indigenous Palestinians.